FLAWLESS

LEADERSHIP

D0175948

Also by Gloria J. Burgess

Books

The Embodiment of Leadership (editor)

Leading in Complex Worlds (editor)

Dare to Wear Your Soul on the Outside: Live Your Legacy NOW

Legacy Living: The Six Covenants for Personal & Professional Excellence

Continuum: The First Songbook of Sweet Honey in the Rock (editor)

Poetry

Journey of the Rose

The Open Door

FLAWLESS
LEADERSHIP

Connecting Who You Are
with What You Know and Do

GLORIA J. BURGESS

Red Oak Press
Edmonds, Washington

Flawless Leadership
Connecting Who You Are with What You Know and Do

Gloria Burgess

Red Oak Press
Edmonds, Washington

Editorial, cover/interior design, and production: Jan Seymour
Author photo: Kevin Ray Smith

ISBN 978-1-892864-03-1

SECOND EDITION
10 9 8 7 6 5 4 3 2
Printed and bound in the United States of America

Table of Contents

Introduction   *xi*
Gratitudes   *xiii*

PART I: The Foundation   *1*

1 Leading Begins from Within   *3*

Who You Are Is the Very Essence of Leadership   *5*
Lead Yourself First So You Can Lead Others   *5*
A Journey of Becoming   *8*
Three Life-Changing Questions   *8*

2 Flawless Leadership   *11*

Faithfulness: The Living Heart of *Flawless Leadership*   *12*
Hope: Another Gift of *Flawless Leadership*   *15*

PART II: WHAT IS UNIQUE ABOUT ME?   *17*

3 Be Grateful   *19*

Gratitude and Our Relationship to People   *20*
Gratitude and Our Relationship to Place   *22*
Gratitude Helps Us Focus   *23*
Gratitude Is Transformational   *24*
Flawless Leadership Practice   *27*

4 Be Yourself   *29*

The Skills You Need to Be Yourself   *30*
Flawless Leadership Practice   *37*

Part III: Who and What Do I Care About?   *39*

5 Be a Servant   *41*

Cultivate an Attitude of Serving Others   *42*
Don't Worry About Who Gets the Credit   *44*
Shift Our Focus   *45*
A Tribal Model of Service   *46*
Values, Beliefs, and Practices of Servant Organizations   *48*
Flawless Leadership Practice   *49*

6 Be Intentional   *51*

Identify Your Values   *52*
Begin with the End in Mind   *54*
Align with Your Purpose   *55*
Be on Purpose, Be the Change   *57*
Flawless Leadership Practice   *58*

7 Be Trustworthy   *61*

The Essentials of Building Trust   *62*
Building Trust One Person at a Time   *67*
Flawless Leadership Practice   *69*

8 Be Courageous   *71*

The Courage to Lead   *72*
The Courage to Serve   *73*
Be Audacious and Daring   *75*
Flawless Leadership Practice   *76*

Part IV: How Will I Channel My Passion to Serve Others?   *77*

9 Be a Dreamer   *79*

Together We Can   *80*
Put Wings on Your Dreams   *81*
The Power of Commitment   *81*
Discern and Clarify Your Vision   *83*
Follow Your Vision, Not Someone Else's   *84*
Make Each Day a Masterpiece   *85*
Flawless Leadership Practice   *86*

10 Be Inspired   *87*

Inspiration Begins with Humility   *88*
Surrendering to the Flow   *88*
Shifting Our Perspective   *89*
Learn from the Spirit of *Ubuntu*   *90*
Flawless Leadership Practice   *93*

11 Be a Learner   *95*

What Does It Mean to Be a Learner?   *96*
Learning Is an Act of Service   *97*
Learning Is About Growth   *98*
Learning Is About Unlearning   *98*
Learning While Crawling on the Floor with the CEO   *99*
Learning Through Play   *100*
Learning from Other Cultures   *101*
Flawless Leadership Practice   *102*

12 Be Persevering   *105*

Don't Ask Why, Ask: *Why Not?*   *106*
Relentless: Lessons from History   *107*
One Leader's Journey to Hell and Back   *110*
Flawless Leadership Practice   *113*

13 Be a Bridge Builder   *115*

Build a Bridge for Others   *116*
Make a Way Where There Is No Way   *118*
How Do You Make a Way?   *119*
Pass It On   *121*
Flawless Leadership Practice   *122*

PART V: CODA   *123*

14 The Journey Continues   *125*

A Poem for Your Journey   *127*
  Song to Myself   *127*
Works Cited   *131*
Resources   *133*
The Author   *137*
Flawless Leadership Resources   *139*
Index   *141*

To all my sisters and brothers
who daily reimagine, repair, and remake our world
into a world we can humbly pass on
to our children, our children's children,
and those who are yet unborn.

Introduction

As a leader in numerous Fortune 100 companies, universities, and philanthropic organizations, I've had the privilege to impact the lives of tens of thousands of people. And as an author, advisor, and speaker on leading and leadership, I've had opportunities to touch the lives of multitudes on six continents.

The golden thread that runs through my work with this diverse spectrum of people is their deep yearning for authentic relationships and their concern for the common good. In my conversations with them, I routinely hear:

> I want to live and work with people who are real. People who are passionate and intentional. People who care about what I care about—dignity and equity for all. People who respect and have reverence for our planet. People who not only value doing, but who also value being.

*   *   *   *   *

Who we are—our being—is paramount.

In 1990, Václav Havel, the first President of post-communist Czechoslovakia, addressed the U.S. Congress. Speaking truth to one of the world's super powers, he said, "Consciousness precedes being, and not the other way around, as the Marxists claim. For this reason, the salvation of this human world lies nowhere else than in the human heart, in the human power to reflect, in human meekness, and in human responsibility."

Havel's remarks stand in stark contrast to how most leaders lead—from the outside in rather than from the inside out. In other words, they value *doing* over *being*. This book offers an alternative perspective, one that prizes being. For as long as we are led by human beings, consciousness about our being must be at the core of how we lead. Indeed, consciousness about being must be central in how we form, equip, and develop leaders. This imperative is what the journey of *flawless leadership* is all about.

Gratitudes

AS THE AWARENESS OF THE IMPERATIVE TO LEAD from within continues to gain momentum in our nations, organizations, communities, and other vital relationships, I feel blessed to stand on the shoulders of pioneers. To these trailblazing women and men and the many others who have affirmed, challenged, and influenced my thinking, writing, teaching, mentoring, and leading, I humbly offer my thanks.

For the inspiration for the title of my book, I extend gratitude to my friend and colleague Peter Block. Many years ago, he wrote *Flawless Consulting*, which addresses the necessity for authentic consultant-client relationships. For years, I've taught the principles and practices of authentic leadership in all kinds of contexts—corporate, health care, IT, media, civic, education, and human services. I do so because I believe all healthy, life-giving relationships are grounded in being—the subject and focus of *Flawless Leadership*.

I'm grateful for wonderful collaborators: Jan Seymour, for her editorial heart and expert skills in excavating and unearthing what matters. Neal, Nikky, and Steve, for believing in me and my voice. My husband John, for his abiding love and partnership; not only does he turn my handwritten drafts into readable pages, he also listens into the heart and soul of my work.

I'm deeply grateful to the people I've worked with for the past 35 years in corporations, institutions, communities, and nations. I am privileged to serve alongside you in my various roles as manager, leader, and advisor. Thank you for entrusting me to support and equip several generations of leaders.

A deep bow to my friend Eva for her generosity of spirit and gracious hospitality. So that I can write undisturbed, she extends the exquisite gift of solitude. While I reside in her secluded island cabin, my typical visitors include rabbits, sparrows, squirrels, wind in the trees, and an occasional deer. Ensconced in a verdant cathedral of old-growth cedars, words and worlds unfurl.

To my fellow leaders—corporate, cultural, citizen, social, and creative artists—thank you for clearing paths, breaking new ground, and building bridges for others who will courageously journey into the wondrous realm of being.

African World Wisdom • Chris Argyris • Angeles Arrien • Howard Behar • Geoff Bellman • Warren Bennis R. B. Blackmon • Ken Blanchard • Peter Block • Lee Bolman • Paul Brainerd • Gwendolyn Brooks • Aja Brown • John Burgess • Quinn Burgess • Skye Burn • Ursula Burns • Julia Cameron Cave Canem • Kevin Carroll • Benjamin Carson • Kevin Cashman • Kenneth Chenault • Ron Chisholm • Lucille Clifton • Johnnetta Cole • Misty Copeland Mihaly Csikszenmihalyi • Robert Crosby • Terrence Deal • Max De Pree • Janet Denhardt • Robert Denhardt • Toi Derricotte • Annie Dillard • Peter Drucker • Cornelius Eady • Marion Wright Edelman • Robert A. Emmons • Medgar Evers • William Faulkner • Nikky Finney • Lillian M. Gilbreath • Mary Jane Gillespie • Daniel Goleman • Martha Graham • Malcolm Guess • Joye Hardiman • Joy Harjo • Judith Jamison • Robert Hayden • Ronald Heifetz • Frances Hesselbein • Langston Hughes • June Jordan • Matthew Kelly • Martin Luther King, Jr. • Coretta Scott King • Jim Kouzes • Anne Lamott • Jan Levy Lee Young-Li • Lester L. Love • Wangari Maathai • Gordon MacKenzie • Barbara Mackoff Nelson Mandela • Wynton Marsalis • Justice Thurgood Marshall • Ruth Massinga • John C. Maxwell • Benjamin Mays • Earnest McEwen, Jr. • Mildred McEwen • Thomas Merton • Michelangelo • Amy Mindell • Arnold Mindell • Maxine Mimms • Ruth Mompati • Thomas Moore • Toni Morrison • Harold Nelson • Henry Nouwen • Naomi Shihab Nye • Hugh O'Doherty • Mary Oliver • Barry Oshry • Jesse R. Otis • Parker Palmer • Nicholas Pennell Sidney Poitier • Barry Posner • Colin Powell • Leontyne Price • Robert Quinn • Lynda Rae Resnick • Adrienne Rich • Eleanor Roosevelt • Sonia Sanchez • Pat Schneider • Donald Schoen • Konji Sebati • Peter Senge • Ken Shelton • Bill Shore • Anne Stadler • William Stafford • Richard Stengel • Sekou Sundiata • Mother Teresa • Howard Thurman • Archbishop Emeritus Desmond Tutu • Cicely Tyson • Derek Walcott • Frank X. Walker • Marvin Weisbord • Evelyn Wemhoff • Margaret Wheatley • Ginny Whitelaw • David Whyte • Serena Williams • Venus Williams • Benjamin Zander • Rosamund S. Zander

To you, my readers, my heartfelt thanks for caring enough to dedicate yourself to life-long learning and growth so that you might share your wealth in the many spaces you inhabit—your family, community, organization, and country.

Our. Time. Is. Now.

Whidbey Island, Washington   Gloria J. Burgess
June 2016

PART I

THE FOUNDATION

The leader for today and the future will be focused on how to be—how to develop quality, character, mind-set, values, principles, and courage.

FRANCES HESSELBEIN

Chapter 1

Leading Begins from Within

*Our being, our personhood, says as much
about us as a leader as the act of leading itself.*

KEVIN CASHMAN

LEADING BEGINS FROM WITHIN. It begins with who you are.

The formation of who we are begins when we are very young, shaping how we live and how we lead. But to fully develop into who you want to be as an individual and as a leader, you must acknowledge who you are *now* and then consciously develop who you are becoming.

That leading begins from within runs contrary to the popular belief that leading begins with what you know or what you do. In fact, of the thousands of books on leading and leadership, most focus on what leaders must know or do to ignite, influence, and inspire others.

Knowing and doing are indeed vital aspects of leading. But these two aspects must be undergirded by being—the inner essence of who we are—as the most fundamental facet of leadership formation and leading.

Each facet of leading—knowing, doing, and being—is critical. In fact, if one facet is muted or missing, the integrity of the whole is compromised, making it impossible to lead in a way that is trustworthy, just, or sustainable.

KNOWING

What you understand.

DOING

What you activate and accomplish.

BEING

Who you are.

This circle is an *Adinkra*, a visual symbol that expresses the essence of leadership in the Akan culture of West Africa. This symbol is called *Adinkrahene* (pronounced ah-DIN-krah-hee-nay) because it is believed to have inspired the design of other visual symbols, signifying the importance of playing a leadership role. I use the symbol throughout the book to inspire your leadership.

We have all experienced leaders who are profoundly knowledgeable, leaders who are adept in getting things done, yet they simply languish in developing themselves as human beings. But in today's wondrously complex, hyper-connected world, it is no longer acceptable to marginalize this necessary dimension of leadership formation and leading, this *being*.

Indeed, if we are to fulfill our promise as enlightened and responsible global leaders, it is essential that we know who we are. Furthermore, it is imperative that we devote ourselves to forming, equipping, and developing leaders from the inside out, and urge them to invest in their own life-long learning.

Who You Are Is the Very Essence of Leadership

In the business world, it's said that culture eats strategy for breakfast. These wise words from management and leadership expert Peter Drucker highlight the supreme significance of culture. Because it creates coherence and cohesion, culture is the vital core of any living system—families, communities, teams, organizations, and nations. Strategy, by contrast, is successful only when it's compatible with and within the context of culture.

The same is true in the realm of leadership.

Who you are is so important, it trumps everything you know and do. Leaders are genuinely successful only when their expression of what they know and do is compatible and congruent with who they are.

Whether you are timid or strong-willed, lacking in self-esteem or supremely confident, you must pay attention to who you are, and who and what you care about. As a leader, who you are is paramount. Who you are—or who you *be*—undergirds and drives everything you know and do.

Who you are defines your leadership walk. Any manager or parent knows that their walk speaks louder than their words. My good friend and former CEO Donna Carlisle puts it this way: "You know when you're in the presence of a real leader. How? Because her walk talks louder than her talk talks." In other words, your leadership walk is the outward demonstration of who and what you value.

Lead Yourself First So You Can Lead Others

The simple truth is that you are born to be a leader. We all are. In fact, you are the most significant leader in your life. However, before you can lead anyone else, you must be able to lead yourself. This is called personal leadership, and it starts and ends with you.

Personal leadership is about taking charge of your own life. It's about realizing that you have the power to control your thoughts, feelings, actions, and reactions. This kind of leadership is about taking responsibility for yourself—including your values, attitudes, and beliefs.

Personal leadership is all about the choices and decisions you make about your life.

The saying that "you are what you eat" not only applies to your physical health, it also applies to your choices and decisions. So, choose and decide wisely. You are the sum total of what you consume and the people with whom you interact. Be mindful about the books and magazines you read, who and what you listen to, what you watch, the photographs and images you have in your home and office, and who you spend time with in your personal and professional life.

Who you are in your daily life informs and shapes who you are as a leader more than any other single factor. Who you are is comprised of your values, attitudes, and beliefs. Your values, attitudes, and beliefs shape your character. Your character drives your choices, affecting who and what you allow into your field of attention. Your values, attitudes, and beliefs also shape *how* you lead, not to mention who will follow or collaborate with you.

And here's the crux of it all. As a leader, what you know and what you do presumes being. It also presumes that you know who you are. That you know who and what you value. That you are aware of your attitudes and beliefs. That you understand that your values, attitudes, and beliefs are connected to and drive your choices.

That's an awful lot of presuming!

Yet, in spite of all this presuming, there are practically no resources available to help you develop this most fundamental and important aspect of leadership—your being.

I wrote *Flawless Leadership* to help fill the gap. I wrote this book as a resource for you—for seasoned leaders as well as for new and emerging leaders.

For seasoned leaders, this book will identify competencies that you probably already possess, but because they are buried within, you don't acknowledge, attend to, apply, or develop them. For new and emerging leaders, this book covers material that you won't find in any standard academic program. Nor will you learn what's covered here on the job in your daily routine of managing and leading.

What *will* you learn? You will learn the value, necessity, and significance of leading from within. You will also learn about the key qualities of being. Not only will these qualities distinguish your contribution as a leader, they will also set you apart from the vast majority of other leaders.

I designed the book to encourage and empower you in your relationships at work, in your community, and in your family. I wrote it to ignite your soul—to light a fire within you that will never be extinguished. A fire that when properly tended will ignite a fire in others.

My friend Dale has this kind of fire. As a volunteer for the American Red Cross, every week he delivers dozens of cartons of donated blood to various local hospitals. For the past 32 years—rain or shine, sleet or snow—he has faithfully delivered this life-giving fluid to help thousands of patients.

Why does Dale serve on behalf of people he will never know? Because that's who he is. Raised during the Great Depression, he knows first-hand what it means and what it takes to live and lead from within, to live and lead from his core values of integrity, respect, and service. A World War II veteran, he knows what it means to serve without any expectation of reward. For Dale, this is simply a way of being, a lifestyle for someone who loves, honors, and values people.

In addition to providing leadership as a Red Cross volunteer, Dale is also a leader in his family, at his church, and in his community. At 93 years old, this former chemical engineer maintains a very active social calendar and is an avid learner. Like all *flawless leaders*, Dale daily demonstrates that he is and will always be a work in progress.

A Journey of Becoming

Learning how to lead is not an event. In other words, learning to lead doesn't have a fixed beginning and ending. Learning to lead is a process that requires countless steps and actions. It is a life-long process. In this sense, learning to lead and leading are about who you are now *and* who you are becoming.

Throughout his long, distinguished career, my mentor and friend Warren Bennis wrote extensively about leadership. In his articles, books, and monographs, he often writes about the process of how leaders are formed, reminding us that above all else leadership is an act of becoming.

Among thought leaders in the field of leadership, Bennis recognized early on that "the process of becoming a leader and the process of becoming a fully integrated human being are one and the same"—both are centered in self-discovery. In other words, leaders don't set out to become leaders. Just like anyone else, they simply set out to live their lives, to express themselves fully.

To express ourselves fully is an invitation to an adventure of a lifetime!

When we accept this marvelous invitation, we do so with the understanding that leading is not only an adventure, it's also a journey. It is a journey of continuous revelation. And on this leadership journey, who you become along the way is far more important than your final destination.

Three Life-Changing Questions

There are over 7 billion persons on the planet. Each one of us is unique in all time. No one else can or ever will be you. Ever. But as unique as we are, we also have a lot in common. And we all want answers to the same fundamental questions: *Who am I? Why am I here? How will I live my life?*

People have asked these life-changing questions throughout the ages. Today's generation is no different. But in today's language, the three questions are articulated somewhat differently:

What is unique about me?

> People who ask this question want to understand their strengths, talents, and opportunities for growth. When you reflect on and answer the question *Who am I?* you will understand what's unique about you. And you will also understand how to channel your energy—your emotional, intellectual, physical, and spiritual assets.

Who and what do I care about?

> When you know who and what you care about, it helps you understand who and what you value. Who and what is of utmost importance to you. When you reflect on and answer the question *Why am I here?* you will understand your life's mission, or purpose. In a word, you will understand your unique why.

How will I channel my passion to serve others?

> No one is an island. We were born to be in relationship. When you truly understand that we belong to one another, you can more fully answer the question *How will I live my life?* In fact, in time this question will evolve so that you ask yourself: *How will I live a life that is worthy of my unique strengths and talents? My unique purpose? My desire to serve others as an agent of transformation?*

Flawless leaders are relentless about asking and living into these life-changing questions. I use each of these questions in the organization of the book's next three sections to introduce you to the key qualities of being that pertain to *flawless leadership*.

What Is Unique About Me?

Chapter 3: Be Grateful

Chapter 4: Be Yourself

Who and What Do I Care About?

Chapter 5: Be a Servant

Chapter 6: Be Intentional

Chapter 7: Be Trustworthy

Chapter 8: Be Courageous

How Will I Channel My Passion to Serve Others?

Chapter 9: Be a Dreamer

Chapter 10: Be Inspired

Chapter 11: Be a Learner

Chapter 12: Be Persevering

Chapter 13: Be a Bridge Builder

Sadly, most of us live our entire lives without ever discovering our unique strengths, our purpose, or how to channel our passion into serving others. That won't happen to you. By reading this book you're investing in yourself so you can answer the questions above and learn more about the qualities of being connected to them.

As you read about these qualities of being, make a mental note of those you already have and want to polish. Also note the qualities you'd like to cultivate, develop, and strengthen. To help you reflect on and incorporate these qualities, I've included a *Flawless Leadership* Practice at the end of Chapters 3 through 13. My hope is that by delving into the questions, qualities, and practices, you will continue to grow and develop into the person and leader you were meant to be.

As you read *Flawless Leadership*, I invite you to underline key ideas. Write in the margins. Doodle. Draw. Whatever you do, add your own thoughts and ideas to make this book a resource that really works for you. My expectation is that you will also mentor others, so that you can pass on what you learn and equip them to do the same.

Chapter 2

Flawless Leadership

Finally I was able to see that if I had a contribution I wanted to make, I must do it, despite what others said. That I was OK the way I was. That it was all right to be strong.

Dr. Wangari Maathai

How is it possible to lead flawlessly? Consciously or unconsciously, flawless leaders aspire to:

- Be authentic in this moment.
- Be a person of integrity in all ways.
- Be genuinely open with and curious about the person they are with.

These dimensions of leading are the foundation of *flawless leadership*, and *flawless leaders* continuously strive to integrate these dimensions into the very ground of who they are.

Even though they continuously aspire to be authentic, be a person of integrity, and be genuinely open and curious, they will occasionally fall short. But they are ever faithful in their quest. Being faithful—constant, diligent, and true—is the living heart of *flawless leadership*.

In the rest of this chapter and the chapters ahead, I'll introduce you to other dimensions of *flawless leadership*. In addition to faithfulness, you'll learn about hope, another important gift of *flawless leadership*. You'll also learn about specific qualities that will take you further into the realm of being.

Faithfulness: The Living Heart of *Flawless Leadership*

Faithfulness includes being faithful to who we are, faithful in hosting our own and others' gifts, and faithful in attending to those who should have a seat at the table but whose access has been institutionally or systematically denied. Faithfulness also includes being gracious stewards of our blessings. This includes recognizing that we are blessed not to hoard or protect our blessings, but that we might be a blessing to others.

Leaders demonstrate faithfulness by believing in a co-worker before she is able or willing to believe in herself. By looking out for the best interests of their organization, their team, and other stakeholders. By consistently choosing to act with integrity in their interactions with their peers.

Years ago I was invited to teach in a graduate program that focused exclusively on the interior realm of leading. The program equipped individuals who desired to become the kind of leader described in this book. Equipped with this knowledge today, I now realize that the entire curriculum focused on the dimension of faithfulness—faithfulness in developing and strengthening the rare yet necessary skills of being authentic, being a person of integrity, and being genuinely open and curious.

Being Authentic

Psychologists and sociologists tell us that authenticity is about being real and genuine. At the end of the day, being real and genuine is about being faithful to what we believe. It is also about being faithful in our actions, choices, and relationships. Grounded in self-awareness, self-knowledge, and self-surrender, leaders who are authentic know their values, and they also know their behavior, choices, and decisions are intimately connected to and congruent with their values.

A leader who demonstrates authenticity allows himself to be open, transparent, and vulnerable with his board members or project team as well as with his children and peers. He is also able and willing to tell the truth and say what's so without blaming, shaming, or judging. The beauty of this kind of truth-telling is its power to disarm others in a way that is quite refreshing and beneficial for all concerned.

In this fresh atmosphere, collaborators will recognize the leader as gardener, one who nurtures and welcomes the bounty and beauty of all voices. One who co-creates cultures of equity and justice, cultures of personal and collective sustainability, cultures where everyone can flourish. In this way, authenticity requires leaders to be accountable—not only to themselves but also to others. As old, outmoded notions of leadership continue to crumble, entire organizations must become more accountable, more hospitable to honoring and hosting the diverse and magnificent gifts of the human spirit.

Being a Person of Integrity

Integrity is the bedrock of leadership. Multi-layered, its strata include alignment, congruence, and honesty as well as ethical and moral intelligence. Leaders with integrity ably and willingly take a stand for who and what they believe in, even when—especially when—it's unpopular to do so.

Integrity also asks leaders to welcome and celebrate the whole of their inner and outer complexity. By being able to honor their own wholeness, they strengthen their capacity to honor others' wholeness. In hosting the magnitude of everyone's emotional, intellectual, physical, and spiritual diversity, leaders send up a flare, igniting that same potential within their institution, organization, or nation.

So that they might discover and appreciate their assets as well as acknowledge their weaknesses and growing edges, integrity calls leaders to be assiduous learners, for they understand that the future belongs to those who prepare for it today.

For leaders who faithfully demonstrate integrity, everything is possible. Leaders who concede their integrity betray themselves, compromise the efforts of those who depend on them, and sabotage the future.

Being Genuinely Open and Curious

Openness is the skill of being able to internally recognize, freely access, and appropriately express feelings and thoughts, without being defensive. In other words, openness is the ability to state what's happening in the moment while it's happening. Although recognizing and openly stating what's happening while it's happening might seem counterintuitive, it's not. This way of being and behaving is actually a very high-level skill, which I'll say more about in Chapter 4.

At a micro-level, the skill of openness indicates that a leader is living and leading from her purpose. Furthermore, this indicator signifies her clear vision of a desired future and her commitment to acting authentically in the moment to bring that vision into fruition. With anyone. Anywhere. Step by step. Day in and day out.

Similarly, engaging associates and team members with genuine curiosity is one of the hallmarks of *flawless leaders*. The skill of curiosity includes letting go of certainty and allowing ourselves to be intrigued, interested, and stimulated by new ideas and perspectives. And also, as I discuss in Chapter 4, curiosity opens the door for discovery, experimentation, and beneficial surprise.

Leaders who are genuinely curious understand that everyone has something to teach them. They greet and chat with the barista at the coffee shop in the same spirit that they greet and chat with peers on their management team.

Not only is the skill of curiosity mutually rewarding on an interpersonal level, it's also beneficial to cultivating a healthy, robust organizational culture. An organization or council that values and encourages curiosity will be rewarded with increased ideation, creativity, diversity in problem-solving and decision-making, productivity, learning, and innovation. Its members and citizens will be more attuned and positively engaged.

Hope: Another Gift of *Flawless Leadership*

Beyond authenticity, integrity, and genuine openness and curiosity, *flawless leaders* offer their associates, allies, and organizations many additional gifts. Chief among them is the vital oxygen of hope.

Tucked inside the boardroom, the CEO of a struggling conglomerate recounts past successes, helping her inner circle remember what it's like to be part of a winning team. Confidently, she invites them to share a story about their strengths. One person's story sparks another's. Slowly, surely, the team's belief in itself is unbanked. And from these now-glowing embers, the fire of hope is rekindled. With hope reignited, the team can focus specifically on what gifts are needed now to reconstitute the organization.

Clearly, being a purveyor of hope requires care, commitment, and choice. *Flawless leaders* care, commit, and choose to lead in a way that is purposeful and intentional. Their leadership style mirrors their lifestyle of being in vibrant relationship with themselves, others, and the world, of embracing an attitude of service—eagerly learning, opening doors, and building bridges for others.

Let's move now to our work of learning to be, learning to *know who you are* so you can be the *flawless leader* that the world needs you to be.

PART II

WHAT IS UNIQUE ABOUT ME? WHO AM I?

Always remember that you are absolutely unique.
Just like everyone else.

MARGARET MEAD

Chapter **3**

Be Grateful

Gratitude is the mother of all virtues.
G.K. Chesterton

For many years Max De Pree, former CEO and chairman of the board of the highly-respected Herman Miller company, has affirmed and influenced how I think about, teach, and practice leadership. An exemplary leader, he has written several influential books about leading and leadership. In them, he has expanded the vocabulary of management and leadership and provided a refreshing vision of what's possible.

In his groundbreaking and insightful book *Leadership Jazz*, De Pree composes an inviting score, noting key qualities necessary for contemporary leaders. Rightly, he begins with gratitude, for this quality of being is at the heart of every meaningful relationship.

Delving into its essence, De Pree reminds us that gratitude is a declaration of dependence. If leaders are dependent on their board members and other constituents, this dependence underscores their mutual connection and responsibility to one another. In this sense, gratitude is the nurturing ground for growing good relationships. Whether they are local or global, he explains that our relationships "are the basis for the actions of a group, team, or organization." Therefore, tending to these relationships is one of the most significant and rewarding tasks of leadership.

Although I didn't realize it until after I'd been a manager for a number of years, gratitude has been and continues to be one of my greatest teachers. Over the years, I've learned that it's not only the nurturing ground for growing good relationships with people, gratitude is also the nurturing ground for all kinds of relationships, including our relationship to place.

Gratitude and Our Relationship to People

Contrary to popular belief, there is no such thing as a self-made woman or man. As Supreme Court justice Thurgood Marshall explains, "None of us got where we are solely by pulling ourselves up by our bootstraps. We got here because somebody—a parent, a teacher, an Ivy League crony, or a few nuns—bent down and helped us pick up our boots."

We all stand on someone else's shoulders. Many shoulders. The shoulders of the people who sacrificed, who paid a price—spiritually and psychologically—for us to be here. I certainly would not be who I am today without the able assistance of teachers, friends, and mentors who listened to my ideas, who whispered an encouraging word in my ear, who supported me along my journey. In all of these ways, gratitude connects me to those who made a way for me. Gratitude even connects me to those who tried to thwart my efforts, those who betrayed me, those who hindered rather than helped me.

Gratitude connects me to generations of people in what used to be the small, rural, segregated town of Oxford, Mississippi where I was born. In an era defined by struggle, resistance, rallies, and protests—mingled with occasional gains—I was surrounded by hatred and bigotry every single day. Back then, Mississippi was considered a good place to be *from*. Today, I'm actually grateful for all the hateful people and horrible things I witnessed and experienced as I came of age during the turbulent Civil Rights Movement, because this negativity sparked the opposite in me, giving me gifts that would shape my future.

I'm also deeply grateful because the people who were engaged in and impacted by this powerful movement for social justice were some of my best teachers, contributing to my spiritual and leadership formation. They infused my life with the spirit of upliftment and possibility that was not available to me elsewhere. I now realize that the poison of prejudice was effectively neutralized by the vigilant people in my personal village—my birth family, church family, and family of neighbors—neutralized by their daily embrace and the cleansing stream of their love and encouragement.

Where would any of us be without a parent, sister, brother, grandparent, or teacher who made time, *just for us?* Do you think you would have the confidence you have today without someone believing in your dreams? Would you be the same person you are today without the people who discouraged you or tried to sabotage your efforts? No. All the individuals you encountered contributed to who you are. Be grateful. Intentionally or not, they helped shape and form you into the person and leader you are today.

Flawless leaders know that people are more precious than anything. These leaders also realize that as precious as people are, they can become even more so because they appreciate in value. People appreciate in value when leaders devote themselves to helping followers and collaborators develop. In this way, leaders intentionally intermingle their DNA with others', which assists in the development of families, organizations, communities, and nations, and in the evolution of humanity.

Gratitude and Our Relationship to Place

As much as we are shaped by the people in our lives, we are also shaped by our environment. Just as I was formed and shaped in the crucible of the Civil Rights Movement as it was played out in both the South and North, you were formed and shaped by your environment—the circumstances, events, and places in your life.

I didn't think much about it then, but I now realize that as I was coming of age, I was practicing a special kind of leadership. Although I didn't have language for it at the time, I was demonstrating servant-leadership. A devoted listener, I was an avid consumer of daily events. Not the news as reported by the media, but the daily events of my own and others' lives.

I devoted countless hours—sitting at the kitchen table, walking along the river bank, gently swaying in an old wooden swing—simply listening as silent witness to my friends' anger, confusion, hurt, and sorrow. In the daily, dehumanizing crush of racism and rejection, I discovered one of my special gifts: the gift of being fully present to others. Offering this gift of full presence to others was transformative not only for me but also for them.

Over the years, I've discovered that we all have something of enormous worth: a powerful gift that comes from within. To cultivate this interior power, *flawless leaders* are intentional about developing themselves from the inside out. They do so not only because they recognize and value themselves, but because they also recognize and value others. *Flawless leaders* also recognize that, by their presence, they can represent a place—an inviting refuge, a safe harbor, a welcome sanctuary.

Reflecting on my experience, I'm deeply grateful for place, for being born into a segregated society in a place that was more hateful than hospitable to African-Americans. Why? Because from those painful, debilitating Mississippi experiences, I also received the marvelous gifts of resolve and resilience. And being part of the Great Migration—the exodus of African-Americans from the South to the North—I was granted the gifts of patience, perseverance, and possibility. I believe all of these gifts have equipped me to live, love, and lead as a wife, parent, community servant, organizational leader, speaker, artist, and mentor.

I believe I've contributed in small yet meaningful measures to the evolution of the people I've met along my way. And as I look back on my experiences and the places I call home, I join with the elders in my personal village, our voices singing strains of that beautiful old spiritual:

> Keep your hands on the gospel plow.
> I wouldn't take nothin' for my journey now.

Gratitude Helps Us Focus

Just as we are grateful for the past and for those who came before us, leaders must also be grateful for the present—for what is right in front of us here and now. Being in the here and now helps to focus our attention.

About the power of focusing and controlling attention, best-selling author and psychologist Mihaly Csikszentmihalyi explains, "To control attention means to control experience." When leaders control their attention, or what they choose to focus on, they control the quality of their own experience and the experience of those around them. In other words, when leaders control what they pay attention to, they actually shape the experience as well as the culture of their team, their congregation, their organization.

In life and in leading, we always have a choice. We can choose to focus our attention on all that can go wrong. The person who darts his car in front of ours and cuts us off in traffic. The co-worker who gets promoted to the job we'd set our sights on. Or... we can focus on all that is going well. The people and moments we can be grateful for today. The people and circumstances we can celebrate.

Many of you have probably heard the insightful teaching story about the two wolves. The version I like best is seen through the eyes of a loving Cherokee grandfather. When his grandson tells his grandfather about a friend who treated him unjustly, the grandfather shares this story with the young boy:

> I, too, have felt great hatred for those who have taken so much, with no sorrow for what they do. But hate wears you down and does not hurt your enemy. Hatred is like taking poison and wishing that your enemy would die.
>
> I have struggled with these feelings many times. It is as if there are two wolves inside me. One wolf is good and does no harm. He lives in harmony with all around him and does not take offense when no offense was intended. This wolf will only fight when it is right to do so, and in the right way.
>
> But the other wolf. Ah! He is full of anger. The littlest thing will set him into a fit of temper. He fights everyone all the time for no reason. He cannot think because his anger and hate are so great. It is helpless anger, for his anger will change nothing.
>
> Sometimes, it is hard to live with these two wolves inside me, for both of them try to dominate my spirit.
>
> Looking intently into his grandfather's eyes, the boy asks, "Which wolf wins, Grandfather?"
>
> With a gentle smile, the grandfather confides, "The one I feed."

The same is true about attention. We can focus on what's wrong in our work or in our life. Or...we can focus on what's right in our world and be grateful for it. Whichever one we choose to feed will grow. It will increase, becoming robust and vibrant. The one we don't feed will lose strength, weaken, and eventually shrink, shrivel, and die.

Gratitude Is Transformational

Our deepest hunger as human beings is our need to be appreciated: we all want to be seen, heard, and know that we belong. Leaders must understand this craving and make it a priority to acknowledge, affirm, and appreciate their associates, collaborators, and followers.

This is important during good times when things are going well, and it is particularly crucial when their organization is struggling or under duress.

Everyone appreciates being acknowledged for their efforts and contributions, appreciated for who they are. Leaders who fail to express their gratitude should not be surprised when their dedicated yet unacknowledged staff find work elsewhere.

Not too long ago, my friend Raj told me he was looking for a new job. A talented, well-respected manager, he seemed to have everything going for him. I asked why he was leaving a position he loved, especially in such a tight job market. Raj shared his discontent about being passed over several times for a promotion. "When I told my boss about my frustration, she basically told me to get in the game."

A quiet, consistently high-caliber contributor, I could tell that my friend was deeply offended by his boss's feedback. "Is there anything else?" I asked.

> What drives me crazy more than anything is that my boss gives credit to everybody on the team but me. I don't know if she doesn't notice or if she just doesn't care. The truth is, I'm really good at what I do, and I'm tired of being taken for granted. I want to work for someone who respects me for who I am and appreciates what I contribute.

Regrettably, Raj's experience is all too common. Yet his experience simply underscores the sad fact that most people don't leave organizations. They leave their bosses.

How might our teams and organizations be different if leaders understood that gratitude is appreciation in action?

In fact, gratitude is one of the most powerful forces on the planet. Why? Because gratitude ignites human beings with the rocket fuel of positivity, propelling individuals and teams into the realm of increased productivity and high performance.

Not only does gratitude ground us in positivity, according to researcher and author Dr. Robert Emmons, gratitude is what gives life meaning. In his intensive research on the new science of gratitude, he and his colleagues have found evidence that parallels what the world's great wisdom traditions have known for thousands of years: gratitude is integral to individual and community well-being, wholeness, and health. For the traumatized, gratitude is also essential for healing.

Furthermore, Dr. Emmons explains, "Gratitude enriches human life. It elevates, energizes, inspires, and transforms." When people cultivate and practice gratitude, they experience many positive, life-giving benefits, including increased energy levels, improved emotional, physical, and spiritual health, and stronger relationships, which can result in stronger teams, organizations, communities, and nations.

Gratitude also dissolves negativity, quelling frustration and fear. Gratitude shuts out bitterness, doubt, and worry because it simply cannot co-exist with darkness and gloom.

Beyond igniting positivity and squelching negativity, gratitude offers us an opportunity to see the world with new eyes, beginning with the world we carry within. In some African households and communities, this lovely blessing is spoken to usher in each new day:

> We bless the elders, for they have come a long way.
> We bless the children, for they have a long way to go.
> We bless the ones in the middle, for they are doing the work.

Replace the word "bless" with the word "thank" and ask yourself: *If I begin each day with a small measure of gratitude, how might the world I carry within me change?*

Know this: if you're unwilling to change the world within, you will not be able to change your relationships, your team, your organization, or the world around you. However, if you commit to change the world within you, you will be able to transform your relationships, your team, your organization, and the world.

Transforming both the receiver and the giver, gratitude's power is profound. Like the sun, gratitude radiates its powerful energy bestowing positive effects everywhere it reaches. Indeed, gratitude actually alters our body's chemistry, literally transforming us from the inside out, which creates a ripple effect, transforming those who are graced by our presence.

Flawless Leadership Practice

Practice being grateful.

Take a moment today to express your gratitude to a parent, teacher, mentor, co-worker, or someone else to whom you want to express your appreciation.

Do it now.

Call him.

Send her a note.

Treat him to lunch.

For the next 30 days, choose a person, place, or moment in time and extend the gift of being grateful. Repeat for the next 30 days. Do it again…for another 30 days. Do it again….

With practice and repetition, you will make the shift from *doing* gratitude to *being* gratitude, integrating it into how you manage your projects or lead your team, integrating it as a way of being, integrating it into your lifestyle as a parent, sibling, or community servant.

You will also learn the deeper meaning of a timeless, universal practice: *walking in gratitude.* Every. Single. Day.

Chapter 4

Be Yourself

In a world where you can be anything, be yourself.

ETTA TURNER

CELEBRATED SCHOLAR AND WRITER JOSEPH CAMPBELL reminds us that "The privilege of a lifetime is being who you are." Helping leaders be who they truly are is my key focus when I coach leaders, my foundational lesson when I teach leadership.

Years ago, I taught in the University of Washington's College of Engineering. I enjoyed teaching the young undergraduate students, but I especially looked forward to teaching the more seasoned students—professional engineers who returned to the classroom to enhance their management and leadership skills.

Before my course, they would complete a series of self-assessments, instruments that provided them with information about their leadership preferences and strengths. If you've been around engineers, you know their tendency to either poke holes in the data or question the process *ad nauseam*. Or both. I quickly learned to begin each course by saying, "I'm going to start with the punch line: the secret to being a good leader is to simply be yourself."

Stunned into silence, the engineers would stare at me for a few moments.

Now that I had their undivided attention, we'd continue. During the course, my students discovered what I'm sharing with you in this book.

For many people, one of the most difficult tasks in the world is to simply be themselves. Why? When we are in our formative years, most of us work very hard to please others—our parents, our teachers, or our Little League coaches. But each time we strive to please others, we give up a little bit of ourselves without realizing it.

Before long, we've morphed into being the person others want us to be rather than being ourselves. Consequently, since many of us don't bother to question or examine our life, we don't even realize that the life we are living is not our own. We don't realize that our identity is based on someone else's notion of who we should be rather than our own. We live from a false self, rather than being who we truly are.

The Skills You Need to Be Yourself

Recently I heard Delta Airlines' president, now CEO, Ed Bastian speak. He talked about organizational culture, specifically focusing on leadership. During his nearly 18 years at Delta, Ed has seen his company's fortunes rise and fall. Like all the major U.S. airlines during the past several decades, Delta's earnings have been buffeted by deregulation, soaring fuel prices, and increasing global competition. During Delta's darkest fiscal period, Ed served as the airline's Chief Restructuring Officer. As the company slid into near bankruptcy, it seemed that only a miracle could pull the airline out of its nosedive towards insolvency and eventual oblivion.

After Ed spoke, he opened the floor for questions. I asked him about those dark days when everyone, including Delta's loyal customers, believed that the company was doomed. In his characteristic, down-to-earth manner, Ed responded by sharing a story with us. To my ears, it sounded like a script for *flawless leaders*.

Though I don't remember Ed's exact words, here's the essence of what he shared:

> We leased an old, dilapidated department store in the heart of downtown Atlanta. This became the "new" Delta headquarters. And every day, we held an open forum for all employees led by members of our executive team. We made it clear that anyone could ask any kind of question and get a straight answer. Even if the answer was, "I don't know, but I'll find out and get back to you."
>
> We intentionally held our meetings in a wide open, dimly-lit area. Because many of our employees had served Delta for decades, we intentionally chose background music from the 1960s and 70s.
>
> The idea behind creating a "cave-like" quality to our meeting space was to clearly communicate to the Delta team that:
>
> > *We*—staff and executives alike—were all in this *together*.
> > *We*—staff and executives alike—were a *community*, where kinship and belonging were paramount.
> > *We*—staff and executives alike—would either sink or swim *together*.
>
> At first, our employees were skeptical. In fact, there were more people peering down into the cave from the floor above than there were people who actually attended our meetings.
>
> But over time, more and more people showed up. With golden oldies music wafting upwards, down the escalator employees came to join our gathering. Why? Because they saw that we (the executives) were serious. We answered each person's questions. If we didn't know, we said so...then we followed up. We listened to their struggles. We shared our own struggles and concerns.

We also shared our hopes and dreams and invited employees to share theirs.

And you know what, ultimately, we shared and celebrated our victory—*together!*

Only leaders who truly understand what it means to "be yourself" can constructively confront and inspire an organization of 80,000 employees, leading them from despairing darkness into the light of expectancy and hope.

I'm grateful to Ed for sharing this story along with other details of Delta's amazing journey. Embedded in his story are those same critical skills that all leaders need, skills that *you* need, skills that will support you in truly being yourself not only as a leader but in all other realms of your life: *self-awareness, openness, transparency,* and *curiosity.*

Self-Awareness

Being yourself begins with self-awareness—the conscious knowledge of your own desires, feelings, motives, thoughts, and traits. This skill also includes the capacity for introspection and reflection.

Flawless leaders understand that developing the skill of self-awareness is essential to becoming a trustworthy leader. They realize that knowing who they are and knowing who and what they care about is crucial to understanding, engaging, and developing meaningful relationships with allies and collaborators. They also recognize that the skill of self-awareness is vital to their ability to ignite, influence, and inspire others.

With sufficient self-awareness, leaders will be better equipped to embrace, reflect on, and use their unique strengths, talents, and gifts. They will be able to recognize what drives them and what gives them energy, focus, and purpose. They will be able to develop and clearly communicate their vision, inspiring their team or organization to meaningful action. They will also be able to leverage their leadership presence and maximize opportunities for growth.

Openness

Openness means being able to internally recognize, freely access, and appropriately express your feelings and thoughts, without being defensive. This sounds pretty straightforward. However, demonstrating this high-level skill can be challenging. In fact, it can be downright difficult. When we're triggered *and* we don't realize it, we can easily respond inappropriately and defensively. In that split second, we become temporarily immobilized; we freeze, which impairs our ability to internally recognize, freely access, and appropriately express our feelings and thoughts, without being defensive. We've all been there.

The key is to develop your ability to self-regulate, so that when you're emotionally triggered, you can consciously manage your own reactivity. Leaders who become proficient in the skill of openness will be able to choose—in the moment—between off-the-cuff, knee-jerk behaviors that thwart their effectiveness and more thoughtful, gracious actions that enhance their relationships and their results.

Leaders who develop the skills of self-awareness and openness are better equipped to understand and reckon with others' reactivity. They can draw on their emotional, social, intercultural, and creative intelligences to understand and relate to team members, customers, vendors, and loved ones.

Just like acquiring any other skill, learning the skill of openness is a process. The process requires commitment, effort, and time. In order to excel at the skill of openness, many of us have to shed old, habitual patterns and learn new behaviors. But most people aren't willing to dedicate themselves to do what it takes to excel. Instead, they settle for average. Setting the bar no higher than the status quo, they only do what's necessary to get by.

On the whole, leaders who settle for average tend to have lower emotional resonance. Why? Because they haven't devoted the energy or effort to develop the kind of skills we're talking about here. Leaders who settle for average give emotionally resonant leaders, those on the way to becoming a *flawless leader*, a competitive advantage, an advantage that propels them to excel to greater levels of responsibility and achievement because, in relation to others, they maximize their contribution, value, and impact for the benefit of all concerned.

Transparency

Transparency allows leaders to make information that is normally selective—seen by only a few—appropriately available to all. Focused on organizational relations, leaders who demonstrate the skill of transparency provide a glimpse behind-the-scenes, providing access to how the organization works. An example is providing insight into the leader's or organization's decision-making processes. Providing such insight can be particularly helpful during times of change and transition.

In one company I worked for, upon learning that we were to be acquired by a rival, the intensely loyal staff was shaken to the core. It appeared as though we'd been blindsided, as if no one had seen this coming. However, senior staff did see it coming, even though they couldn't reveal specifics until after the acquisition was complete. Afterwards, the leadership team provided frequent opportunities for communication, such as live forums to discuss how decisions had been made and were being made going forward. They also provided daily FAQs, which helped enormously.

The skill of transparency can also be applied to team and inter-team relations. In almost every organization, teams that should be working together aren't. Instead, they are cut off from one another, each team working in their own silo.

Silos exist for many reasons. Sometimes, they exist because they're necessary for a team to do its best work. For example, a "tiger team" or "skunk works" or "special operations" team, working on an ad hoc, time-limited project. Often silos exist simply because people feel more at ease with people they work with the most.

Because many organizations rely on multiple teams to create, launch, and deliver their products and services, silos can and do get in the way. Transparency can facilitate team, inter-team, and organizational success. Examples of transparency include providing insight into a team's mission and norms or providing key information on their priorities, schedules, or workflow.

One of my team members is fond of reminding me that "information is the solar energy of an organization." In other words, even a little transparency will go a long way. Imagine what a lot can do.

The need for transparency has never been greater. As old, outworn containing structures and hierarchies dissolve and as organizations struggle to survive, *flawless leaders* will be equipped to fill the void. In a world where ambiguity and chaos are the norm, these leaders will be equipped to support their organizations to adapt, innovate, and flourish. Followership, collaboration, and alliances depend on people at all levels who are self-aware, open, and transparent.

Curiosity

Leaders who are curious are inquisitive, avid learners who desire to learn or know more. They vigorously cultivate, nurture, and leverage the skill of curiosity.

Even though we're naturally curious as children, as we grow older we may not necessarily retain our curiosity. Not only did my dad want me to retain my curiosity, he wanted to ensure that I cultivated and developed it. When my family moved from rural Mississippi to the inner city of Detroit, Michigan, we lived in some very rough neighborhoods. During the hot, humid summers, instead of playing outside with the other kids, I had to go to school. Unlike most kids who attend summer school because they flunked a course, I went to summer school because my dad mandated it. He was the headmaster, our house was the classroom, and my sisters and I were the pupils.

Every day while our friends played outside our house in the street or their yards, we completed our daily lessons. We studied hard to pass the tests that dad administered after dinner. During those Detroit summers and for years afterwards, I remember asking my dad about particular words or concepts that interested me.

Invariably, he said, "Look it up."

Can I just tell you, this is *not* what a young person wants to hear. But, dutifully, I always followed my father's advice.

Was my dad being mean? I admit that's what I thought, though I had the good sense to keep it to myself!

So, what was he doing? My dad was helping me cultivate an appetite for curiosity. He was instilling in me the awareness, knowledge, skills, and resourcefulness for life-long learning. And you know what? It worked. I became very good at being curious and quite skilled in satisfying my curiosity. In fact, I became a voracious learner. The more I learned, the more I wanted to learn. And the more curious I became.

As a visual learner, I was adept at memorizing words and their definitions. I was fascinated to learn that some writers had a knack for arranging words in such a way that their work came alive, while other writers were just downright boring. Although I didn't realize it at the time, I was learning about the writer's voice, tone, and style. Looking up words and other concepts stimulated my thinking, fueled my appetite for learning, and spurred my life-long curiosity.

Cultivating the skill of being curious also expanded my world far beyond the one I knew—the six-square blocks of my neighborhood in East Detroit. Being curious, along with other qualities of being, has opened doors and opportunities to build relationships, work with, and serve people in over 30 countries on six continents.

*   *   *   *   *

The skills of *self-awareness, openness, transparency,* and *curiosity* are the foundation stones for developing personal mastery. Each skill is distinct. Each skill is essential. Each one builds on itself and the others. Together they work in concert to support you in being who you truly are.

Flawless Leadership **Practice**

Practice being yourself.

Being yourself can be challenging. So many of us focus on pleasing others. In the process, we lose track of who we are along the way.

That's a steep price to pay.

Fortunately, there are many ways to get back on track with being who you are meant to be, to discover your strengths as well as your growing edges.

Begin by asking yourself a few questions.

What's unique about me?

What are my top three strengths?

What do I enjoy doing so much that I lose track of time?

What do I enjoy so much I would do it for free?

What am I curious about?

By taking time to answer these few questions, you will learn more about who you are *and* plant the seeds for your personal and professional growth. Your responses are just the beginning to a life-long adventure.

PART III

WHO AND WHAT DO I CARE ABOUT? WHY AM I HERE?

The essence of leadership is not giving things or even providing visions, it is offering oneself and one's spirit.

LEE BOLMAN & TERRENCE DEAL

Chapter **5**

Be a Servant

We must learn before we can prepare.
We must prepare before we can serve.
We must serve before we can lead.

William Arthur Ward

Above all else, the leader's role is defined by being a servant.

But how do we equip leaders to serve?

Much has been written about the key qualities of servant-leaders, yet it's hard to imagine anyone who understands what it means and what it takes to be a servant better than those who choose to serve in the military. Perhaps this is because they have pledged to pay the ultimate price of laying down their lives. For the men and women who devote their lives to military service, their desire to serve is simply a way of being, a way of life.

Many years ago, my friend Gary joined the U.S. Air Force. Recently he shared that his desire to serve his country goes back as far as he could remember. "Long before I discovered success in any real sense, I discovered the value of service. Early on, I learned that the principle of service is closely related to the law of sowing and reaping." This universal law basically says that as we render service to others, we plant the seeds of all that is good — compassion, generosity, knowledge, and wisdom — and we reap rewards in at least equal proportion to the amount of our service.

Cultivate an Attitude of Serving Others

As Gary discovered the value of service, he learned to value serving. He also learned that being a servant requires us to cultivate an attitude of serving and that our return for serving others can take many forms.

Having a desire to serve and being equipped to serve are quite different. Not only did Gary desire to serve when he enlisted, the Air Force effectively equipped him to do just that.

> Something happens to a man when he commits to serving his country through military service. I've seen the stark differences in a young recruit between the day they depart for and the day they return from basic military training. I've experienced those changes myself and give credit to military service for the lessons I've learned and the rewards I've enjoyed as a result.
>
> The very real lessons of never leaving a wingman behind are ingrained from the start and are often tested in the daily regimen of a military lifestyle as well as on the battlefield. Along with all the training, discipline, and protocol are the values of teamwork, integrity, and service before self.

As an airman, Gary learned lessons in personal growth, commitment, discipline, and teaming. These lessons can be applied in any area of life, and especially to leading and leadership.

If you're thinking that the process of equipping leaders to be servants in sectors other than the military can be tricky business, you're right. Why? Serving others has often been described as a way of helping others get what they want—*and*—that by doing so, you can get what you want. But this view of serving misses the point. Helping others in order to get what you want is *not* why you serve.

Flawless leaders serve because they value helping and serving others; they are primed to serve not as something they *do* but as an integral aspect of who they *are*. For them serving is as vital and natural as breathing. Driven by a relentless sense of ethical and moral responsibility, *flawless leaders* are committed to cultivating and infusing an attitude of service for themselves and throughout their organizations, communities, and families.

Born into a family that values helping and serving, my friend Grace Stanley is 14 years old. Her dream is to end human trafficking, a dream that was ignited when she was 12. When I spoke with Grace, I immediately realized that she was no ordinary young woman.

Grace is a leader. Not only does she have a burning desire to serve others, she has already launched her own organization to focus on raising awareness and safety regarding human trafficking. When I asked how she came up with her idea, she explained, "My first experience [with human trafficking] was in 2014."

That summer as Grace sat in her living room, she heard about the nearly 300 Nigerian girls who were abducted and targeted to be sold into sex trafficking. After conducting her own research, she learned that trafficking was rampant in the U.S., "smashing [her] assumption that it was only in the third world." She was also confronted with many stark statistics, including the harsh reality that although 85 to 95 percent of the women, men, and children ensnared in human trafficking want to escape, few ever do. Then and there, Grace decided to take a stand.

As CEO of Missing Petals, the organization she formed to raise awareness about human trafficking, Grace realizes that she can't achieve her dream alone. Her goal is to partner with other like-minded organizations to raise awareness and ultimately to eradicate human trafficking.

Like other *flawless leaders*, Grace understands what it means and what it takes to be a servant. For her, being of service is as necessary as air.

Don't Worry About Who Gets the Credit

Exemplars of service include Mahatma Gandhi, Mother Teresa, Albert Schweitzer, Ellen Johnson Sirleaf, Eleanor Roosevelt, and Dr. Martin Luther King, Jr. It's actually ironic that we even know the names of these leaders, ironic because these leaders with a heart for being a servant didn't care about who got the credit. They simply wanted to serve their countries, communities, and fellow human beings.

On a personal level, this selfless view of service was made even more vivid when my husband John and I had the good fortune to visit South Africa. Pearl, a friend of a mutual friend, volunteered to be our host. She wanted to personally ensure that John and I had an authentic experience of her beautiful homeland. Why? "Because," she assured us, "that is the spirit of true South Africans."

During the months leading up to our visit, Pearl took great care in making arrangements for us to meet and stay with families of different political, racial, and socio-economic backgrounds. She also set aside time to fly from her adopted home country of Switzerland to South Africa to accompany us during our visit and serve as our personal guide. She especially wanted to escort us to several historical sites. One of them was Robben Island, the infamous prison off the coast of Cape Town where Nelson Mandela served 27 years as a political prisoner.

A hero to many, including me, Mandela is one of the few contemporary statesmen who deeply understood and exemplified service. In my book *Dare to Wear Your Soul on the Outside*, I write about the legions of South African women whose stand against the powerful white government helped dismantle their horrific system of apartheid. Akin to these courageous women, Mandela was driven to right past injustices, fueled by an attitude of service without worrying about who got the credit.

Thanks to her servant attitude and personal care, Pearl gave us an enormous gift: John and I experienced the impact of two of South Africa's selfless leaders—the rich legacy of Mandela's servant-leadership as well as the kindness, generous hospitality, and servant-leadership of our host.

Shift Our Focus

Throughout history and in all cultures, to be a servant is to put others first.

But what does it mean to be a servant in contemporary contexts? How glibly we call ourselves global citizens, metrocultural and multifaceted. Yet deep schisms exist in how we imagine and engage in service.

At a very basic level, some cultures are focused more on "we" than "I." Generally speaking, we-focused cultures are more oriented and attuned to the collective; I-focused cultures are more oriented and attuned to the individual. Both we-focused and I-focused cultures have much to learn from one another. Most essentially, that each is here not to have dominion over the other, but to value, honor, and serve one another.

Flawless leaders understand that just as they have been served by the women and men on whose shoulders they stand, they have a responsibility to serve others. To walk beside them. To partner with them. To be genuinely curious and not blindly impose themselves or their ways of knowing, thinking, and being on others.

By 2045, the world will be very different than it is today. Our population will increase by almost 30 percent—from 7 billion to 9 billion. Not only will there be more persons on the planet, in some countries, the population will shift from being predominantly white to being predominantly persons of color. Also, between now and 2045, a significant percentage of the population will experience some kind of dislocation—due to geo-socio-political shifts, war, depletion of resources, and extreme natural disasters. In ways that we cannot predict or even fathom, many of us will experience disruption of life as we know it today.

It behooves leaders to be proactive in shifting their focus so they can situate themselves to rethink, reconsider, and reimagine our world, our nations, and our organizations. Ask yourself: *What might I learn about serving and service from traditions and cultures different than my own?*

A Tribal Model of Service

When I worked in the philanthropic sector, I had the privilege of leading teams and partnering with others to design and deliver leadership development programs in a variety of geographical, social, and cultural contexts. One of my favorite assignments was serving in Southeast Alaska where I worked with elder and emerging leaders in the Tlingit and Haida Indian tribes.

Each gathering began with prayer—a wonderful and generous practice of extending gratitude and nourishing the heart and soul of community. Our hosts posted their tribal values on the walls of our gathering place, reminding me and other guests of what held significance.

To my eyes, these tribal values express the Tlingit's and Haida's deep reverence for service. Their values also define a people, a way of being, a way of living, an honorable way of serving one another and all relations, a way of leading within the context of their tribal community and beyond.

In the values of the Tlingit and Haida, I find that many of them correspond with the values of communities, families, and organizations I'm familiar with in North America and throughout the world. Not surprisingly, the value of serving others consistently shows up.

SOUTHEAST ALASKA TRADITIONAL TRIBAL VALUES

"OUR WAY OF LIFE"

- Discipline and Obedience to the Traditions of Our Ancestors

- Respect for Self, Elders, and Others

- Respect for Nature and Property

- Patience Always

- Pride in Family, Clan, and Traditions as Found in Love, Loyalty, and Generosity

- Strength in Mind, Body, and Spirit

- Humor in All Things

- Support for Each Other

- Good and Respectful Listener

- Careful Speaker

- Stewards of the Air, Land, and Sea

- Reverence for Our Creator

- Peaceful and Harmonious Life

- Strength and Courage

Values, Beliefs, and Practices of Servant Organizations

I've made a composite list of the values, beliefs, and practices of servant organizations. As you read my list, consider your own. What would you add, omit, or amplify?

- Above all, appreciate people—nurturing them is a spiritual mandate.

- Take good care of people, and they will take good care of themselves, their families, our customers, our community, and beyond.

- Listen closely…to our customers, vendors, competitors, detractors, enemies, and champions.

- Everyone succeeds or no one does.

- Each one, pull one: we are all in this together.

- Celebrate team victories, not your own.

- Keep learning and growing—always and in *all* ways.

- Maximize our strengths while keeping our knees bent, allowing us to recognize and seize new opportunities.

- Take care of ourselves—emotionally, intellectually, physically, and spiritually—as the ultimate act of generosity towards the future.

- Welcome diversity—for diversity fosters creativity, a strategic resource for organizations and nations.

In addition to valuing and practicing service, great companies, communities, and nations share kindred perspectives on the true nature of success. These organizations, citizenries, and governments would agree that true success comes from honoring the dignity and valuing the contribution of every person. Wise leaders also recognize that if one voice is missing or muted, the integrity of the whole suffers— everyone and everything is compromised, diminished.

Flawless Leadership Practice

Practice being a servant.

To serve in our families and other key relationships is no different than being a servant in our boardrooms, classrooms, and meeting rooms.

Choose one thing from the list below and practice it today.

VALUE OTHERS

In serving, we must remember to:

Be humble.

Nourish others.

Offer to help, assist, and stand in.

Ask, not tell.

Ask: *What's important to you?*

Ask: *How can I be of use? How can I serve you?*

Learn another language or two…maybe three or four.

Lead from the side.

Lead from behind.

Give up being a sage on the stage.

Be a guide.

Be an ally.

Be a coach.

Be a mentor.

Not worry about who gets the credit.

Know when to follow.

Know when to flip the script and be a learner.

Use silence as a resource.

Practice the same thing again tomorrow.

Keep practicing for an entire week. Notice what happens. Don't judge yourself...just notice.

Now choose something else from this list—something that will be a stretch for you. Practice it for a week—with friends and family. Then practice an additional 21 days with your team and other co-workers. As you do, notice what happens. Don't judge yourself...just notice.

Jot notes to yourself about your experience.

Bravo!

Keep serving.

Keep practicing.

Be Intentional

How we spend our days is, of course, how we spend our lives.

ANNIE DILLARD

WHEN WE LIVE WITH INTENTION, WE WILL LEAD with intention. *Flawless leaders* are intentional so that they can be of highest and best service to themselves and those they serve.

Being intentional is choosing, consciously and daily, activities and actions that align with your purpose. Of course, this assumes that you already know your purpose just as you know your team's purpose and your organization's purpose. Like nested Russian dolls, all these purposes should fit together, ensuring that everything works together for good—for you, your family, your team, your organization, your community, and your nation.

You may not realize it, but your daily choices and actions are driven by your values. Your values shape your attitude, govern your beliefs, and mold your character. When you surface your values and make them conscious, like a powerful force field they will support you in living and leading with intention.

Identify Your Values

As McKesson's chairman, president, and CEO John Hammergren explains, "Whether you're talking about a person or a company, leadership is about values." Although it's important to identify your values, to make them visible, many people have never done so. Amazingly, most people spend more time shopping for a new car or new pair of shoes. I've coached, developed, and taught leaders for years, but I'm still surprised to discover how few of them have taken the time to identify their values. Or, if they have, how few really reflect on them.

Identifying your values is vital not only for you, but also for your organization.

So how do you identify your values? One of the best ways is to ask yourself a series of questions with the understanding that the process will be iterative, and that it's a process you can revisit throughout your life:

> *Do I value myself?* When you value yourself, you have what it takes to value others.
>
> *Do I value others?* When you value others, you naturally want to serve them.
>
> *Do I regularly ask myself how can I serve others?* Ask this question daily and it will become a habit, a way of being.
>
> *Who are the three people I most admire and respect?* You can only see in others what is already a part of you.

What specific qualities of being do these people exhibit that warrants my admiration and respect? Jot down the specific qualities. Why? Because if you can see it, you can be it.

What three things do I care about more than anything else? Knowing what you care about will help you prioritize how you express and renew your emotional, intellectual, physical, and spiritual energy.

If I could change anything in the world, what one thing would I change? Knowing what you would change will help you be more intentional about focusing your attention, energy, and time.

What is the source of my joy? Joy comes from within. True joy comes from the satisfaction of being content with and faithful to who you are.

Who or what do I love more than anything in the world? Above all else, who or what you love defines who you are.

What makes me sing? What makes me cry? Knowing what makes you sing and what makes you cry tells you what you are passionate about. Passion combined with purpose is unbeatable and unstoppable.

What do I stand for? A person who stands for nothing will fall for anything. When you know what you stand for, silence is not an option.

Knowing your values provides meaning and shape to your life. Being grounded in your values provides a stable foundation for living and leading with intention. Everything rests on this foundation. It gives you a solid place to stand and provides support for all of your aspirations in your relationships, health, finances, work, and spiritual life.

When we fail to live and lead in congruence with our values, we are at the mercy of other people. It's very easy to get swept up in *their* agenda rather than staying true to and in harmony with our own direction and purpose.

Begin with the End in Mind

In addition to providing a solid foundation, knowing your values is essential to creating your personal purpose statement. If you've never taken the time to discern and identify your purpose, one way forward is to begin with the end in mind.

Beginning with the end in mind is a commitment to be intentional about taking charge of yourself. Start by answering these questions: *What is unique about me?* and *Who and what do I care about?*

When you identify your uniqueness and who and what you care about, it will give you a stronger sense of who you really are. In other words, it will give you a stronger sense of self. In advising both seasoned and emerging leaders, American Express CEO Kenneth Chenault says, "Have a strong sense of self. Without it, you cannot lead." Moreover, "You risk being consumed by all sorts of elements that don't reflect what you're about."

In addition to having a strong sense of self, *flawless leaders* are faithful to prioritize building themselves from the inside out. Chenault explains:

> There has always been a focus on the rational aspects of leadership and the intelligence required of leadership. I think [both are] absolutely essential. But what I have seen in companies throughout my career is that if you are not clear on who you are, on what it is you stand for, and if you don't have strong values, you are going to run your career off a cliff.

When you begin with the end in mind, you will have a reliable compass to guide you in your daily choices and activities. People who don't begin with the end in mind tend to be pulled in whatever direction seems exciting at the time. However, when the excitement wanes, they muddle about with no sense of direction at all. Rather than following their own North Star, they're pulled by the force of *anybody's* star.

Creating a personal purpose statement will help you stay focused so you can properly channel your energy into what matters to you. Your personal purpose statement should answer the question *Who and what do I care about?* Your personal purpose statement will:

Provide clarity, which will give you a clear, compelling image of what's important to you.

Provide direction, which will allow you to be intentional, to purposefully focus your unique gifts and channel your passion.

Provide meaning, which will allow you to be intentional about living and leading from your purpose, so you can make the difference that only you can make.

Ultimately, as you develop, fine tune, and work with your personal purpose statement, it will help you discover that, as Mark Twain noted, the two most important days of your life are the day you were born and the day you realize why. Leaders discover their why when they know who they are, when they know who and what they care about.

When leaders don't know their why, they can easily lose their way, which is precisely what happened to my client Jin.

Align with Your Purpose

When Jin and I began our coaching relationship, she was a senior leader in a very large healthcare services company. In the early months of working together, Jin experienced episodes of illness that left her physically and emotionally drained. Over a period of several months, her episodic illness increased in frequency and duration, culminating in a physical breakdown that rendered her incapacitated for several weeks. In parallel with her illness, Jin began to reflect on her purpose and how it was connected to her work. Or not.

Shaken by her unexpected breakdown, Jin was also gratified by what could only be called a miraculous breakthrough. As she discerned her purpose, she came to realize that it was not in sync with her work. With this new awareness, Jin experienced a new sense of liberation and recommitted herself to being intentional about attending to her emotional, intellectual, physical, and spiritual health. Over the next year, Jin made steady progress towards her goal while gaining more perspective and clarity about her purpose.

During a recent coaching session, I asked Jin how things were going and if she had anything specific she'd like to share. To track her goals and progress, Jin keeps a journal. Joyously, she shared the following excerpt with me:

January 20

My heart is overflowing with thanksgiving today! I'm well physically, mentally, and spiritually. Lord, thank you for healing me!

Three days ago, I fell down the stairs. It compounded my recent muscle spasm episode. I had trouble sitting for too long and getting in and out of a car. So I soaked in a bath and used the heating pad. It helped a lot, but I was still sore. I prayed and visualized God placing His hand on the spot that was sore. My muscle relaxed, and wow...the pain went away just like that.

Yesterday, my hips were looser than before the fall. I had more energy in everything I did. Hmmmm...I'd carried a lot of tension in my hips, shoulders, and neck, which made me sick, lethargic, and unmotivated.

My newfound energy and "freedom" has given me the courage to do whatever I want. During the quarterly review [at work] yesterday, I was a strong leader. I didn't worry about what others might think. I acted in harmony with my spirit.

In sharing her light bulb moment, Jin said, "Wow, that's the key, isn't it? When we're stressed, we're not in unity with our spirit. Today, I strive to be one with my spirit! I will strive to be free!" Chuckling, she said, "Gloria, although we'd discussed this before, this time it really hit home."

In addition to deepening her commitment to make more time for self-care, Jin also gained a deeper appreciation for what being faithful means in her life. Most significantly, her insights were intimately connected to her life's purpose.

Be on Purpose, Be the Change

Most people want to make a difference in the world, but they don't have a clue about how to *be the change* to make this happen. Faced with so many options, some people are unsure where to begin or where to focus their energy for maximum effect. Some people are overwhelmed by the mere thought of making a difference. Some simply lack sufficient awareness about who they are and who and what they care about. In short, they lack awareness about their purpose.

This was certainly true of Nelson Mandela. Long before he understood his purpose, the young boy whose birth name Rolihlahla meant "trouble maker" had no idea what lay ahead of him. He had no idea of his destiny. Even so, Nelson Mandela's long walk to gain freedom for his country and himself was characterized again and again by intention. How can that be? We can't always connect the dots in our life by looking forward. Sometimes, life makes sense as we look back on it. When we live and lead faithfully, we trust in advance what will only make sense in reverse.

Like all of us, Mandela's leadership formation began when he was very young. Nurtured by his father Gadla Henry Mphakanyiswa until his untimely death and later by his Uncle Jongintaba, both men were tribal chiefs. When young Nelson went to live with his uncle, the chief was the acting king of the Thembu people. Little did Mandela know that he was being formed for his purpose.

While attending university, Mandela experienced a moment of truth, a moment that would define his life. After being elected to become a member of the Student Council, he refused the office.

Because only a small percentage of the student body had voted, Mandela told the authorities that without the students' support, he would not take a seat on the council. Although he was threatened with expulsion, he stood his ground, refusing to change his mind. Ultimately, the authorities relented; Nelson remained in school. This seemingly insignificant event was a hallmark of Mandela's strong ethical and moral values.

Years later, Nelson Mandela would be elected into his country's highest office, elected by a vote that for the first time included all the people of South Africa. Of the 21.7 million eligible voters—about 16 million had never previously voted due to apartheid laws that did not allow them to—more than 19.7 million voted in this historic election. Even Mandela voted for the first time in his life.

*   *   *   *   *

Flawless leaders are intentional. They know their values. Every day they stand on their values. As they move through their tasks and responsibilities, their choices and actions are based on their values and on a deep, abiding faithfulness to their purpose.

Flawless Leadership Practice

Practice being intentional.

Flawless leaders are grounded in their values. They also understand their unique strengths and know their purpose. With this awareness, they can creatively and intentionally engage in their own work and proactively interact with others.

What values guide your daily actions and choices? Write down two or three of them.

If you don't know your values, make a point to discover them. It's important for leaders to know what drives them. Be intentional. Make an appointment with yourself. Put it on your calendar. Then...tell someone. Not just anyone. Tell someone who will be an accountability partner for you.

To identify your values, you can use the questions in this chapter to guide you. If you feel stuck, reach out to someone in your company—in HR, Talent Management, or Training and Development—and ask about resources they'd recommend.

When you've identified your values, see how they line up with how you spend your time and energy. Don't judge yourself. Just notice.

Know that this is a process. Adjust and tune as needed. Be intentional.

Over time, you will align your values, choices, and actions.

When you stray off course, be intentional to realign yourself.

Repeat as needed.

Chapter 7

Be Trustworthy

Trust is built and maintained by many small actions over time.
LOLLY DASKAL

WHEN A LEADER HAS TRUST, EVERYTHING IS POSSIBLE. Without trust, nothing is possible.

So, what does it mean to be trustworthy?

Being trustworthy has many layers and nuances. Ultimately, trustworthiness is grounded in our values, which become evident through our behavior. Being trustworthy is about the leader's choices and actions—their behavior—*and* it's also about followers' perception of the leader's behavior. In this sense, trustworthiness is a two-way street.

To demonstrate that they're worthy of our trust, leaders faithfully attune to themselves and others. In their encounters and experiences with others, they thoughtfully construct and diligently reinforce what they say and do. In other words, they take care to make sound choices, notice how their choices affect others, and tune their behavior as necessary.

Becoming a person who is worthy of trust takes time. It doesn't happen overnight. Becoming trustworthy is a process that occurs gradually through a long progression of meaningful and sometimes not so meaningful encounters and experiences with others. An integral aspect of an individual's formation, this process begins long before a person assumes the responsibilities and tasks of leadership.

While earning and sustaining trust requires specific choices by the leader, it also requires something from followers. In their encounters and experiences with their leader, followers interpret and evaluate their leader's choices and actions. Not once. Not twice. But over and over again. Why? For followers, trusting their leader also takes time.

Just as becoming trustworthy is a process, being willing to trust their leader is also a process. For followers, this process happens over time through a long progression of moments, encounters, and experiences with their leader. During this process, followers assess the leader's trustworthiness—continuously. How? By internally asking two questions: *Are you competent?* and *Are you looking out for my best interests?* In other words, *do you care?*

The Essentials of Building Trust

To earn and sustain trust leaders must not only demonstrate *competence* and *caring*, they must also demonstrate *character* and *consistency*. *Flawless leaders* demonstrate these qualities by connecting who they are with what they know and what they do.

Competence

Competence is about successfully and proficiently applying what you know.

People naturally rally around leaders who make things happen, leaders with the ability—in terms of awareness, knowledge, skills, and resources—to get things done properly and effectively. Followers and allies want to partner with leaders who have the energy, stamina, and perseverance to accomplish goals and achieve results.

Leaders depend on and are open to the competence of their associates. Xerox's chairwoman and CEO Ursula Burns is the first African-American woman of a Fortune 500 company to have achieved this rank. In terms of demonstrating competence in working with her peers and others, Burns says, "I didn't learn to be quiet when I had an opinion. The reason they knew who I was is because I told them." Fortunately, her peers and other leaders at Xerox were open to Burns' competence.

Beyond technical, managerial, and leadership knowledge and ability, we also want to know if leaders have the competence to be faithful to their followers, allowing the gifts of followers to surface and shine. In other words, followers and other allies want to know if their leader will trust them and others to do what their leader can't or shouldn't do. *Flawless leaders* ask themselves: *What is mine to do?* In other words, *What can I not delegate?* In this way, they also ask: *How might I encourage or support others in offering their gifts?*

Caring

Caring is about looking out for the best interests of others.

One of the most important responsibilities for leaders is to cultivate and establish relationships. Like a good gardener, leaders must also tend and nurture their relationships. When relationships tear, they must repair them. To keep them fresh and vibrant, they must renew their relationships. Followers welcome such leaders.

According to leadership and relationship expert John Maxwell, before they give a leader their trust, followers, partners, and collaborators internally ask: *Do you care about me?* and *Can you help me?* Both are questions about relationship.

We all want to be in relationships with people who care about us and who can help us. Even so, occasionally we encounter people who don't get it or who just don't care. Unfortunately, sometimes those people are our bosses.

Years ago when I was in the IT industry, I worked for the technology division of Bank of America. My manager's name was Dan. After flying to Michigan to attend my father's funeral, I requested Dan's approval to stay an extra week to help my mom with the myriad details that accompany the death of a loved one.

When I arrived back in my office, the first thing Dan said to me was, "How's that project coming along? I need your report and updated project plan by noon today." At this time in my career, I'd worked in high tech long enough to know not to expect warm fuzzies from my boss—or anybody else for that matter. But I did expect him to say, "Hello" or "How are you doing?" or "How's your family?" or "How's your mom?"

My dad and mom mean the world to me, and it was very painful to lose my dad and witness my mom's grief. Rather than raise the roof with Dan, I simply raised my eyebrows, went to my cubicle, and dove into my work. Along with my project report and updated project plan, I also submitted my resignation. And I delivered all of them to Dan's desk before noon.

Caring matters.

Character

Character is about who you are on the inside.

Leaders reveal their character by their choices, actions, and decisions. Allies and collaborators want a leader to be who he says he is. What he does must match what he says. In other words, his walk and talk must be aligned. Moreover, his walk and talk must match at home, at work, at the gym, and at the grocery store. My friend and former Starbucks executive Howard Behar calls this his "One Hat Theory of Leadership."

When a leader's values, choices, and behaviors are congruent no matter where she is or who she's with, we see her as trustworthy. When a leader's values, choices, and behaviors don't line up, we say she's "dubious," "fickle," "flaky," "questionable," "two-faced." All of these are simply code terms for untrustworthy. For leaders who make the headlines because of their untrustworthy behavior, we brand them as conniving, corrupt, deceitful, shady. They lack character.

U.S. General H. Norman Schwarzkopf defined leadership as "a potent combination of strategy and character." But he wisely cautioned, "If you must be without one, be without strategy." In other words, character trumps everything.

People with character give up their right to be untrue and unprincipled.

Consistency

Consistency is about reliability in your choices, actions, and relationships.

Leaders who are reliable demonstrate that they can be counted on to show up, make sound decisions, perform, and get results. And leaders must demonstrate that they can be counted on—not once in a while but over and over, day in and day out.

Flawless leaders demonstrate reliability in their relationships by consistently thinking, choosing, and acting in terms of and on behalf of the whole. For example, when making a decision that affects the company's products or sales, they consider the ripple effect on all stakeholders—other departments, business units, suppliers, customers, investors, their community, our planet. They also consider whether their voice is even necessary because they are keenly aware that adding their voice can unnecessarily amplify it, raise the stakes, or make it more difficult for others to act.

Leaders must also consistently demonstrate their respect for others. Like my friend Raj who you met earlier, followers want to know if their leader sees them, if their leader respects them. Show them that you do, and your followers will see you as a leader who is worthy of *their* respect.

Flawless leaders realize that no one is perfect or perfectly consistent, including themselves. Although we usually think of respect as admiring someone or holding them in high esteem, respect also means to look back on, to look again. When leaders admit their mistakes, they show their vulnerability, affording followers an opportunity to look again. Leaders usher fresh air into their relationships when they say, "I'm sorry, I overlooked that." Or, "It's my fault. I sometimes shoot before I aim. I apologize." Or, "Will you coach me so that won't happen again?" Such leaders earn our respect. By being vulnerable, they allow their followers to see them in a new light.

Followers understand that we all make mistakes and we're all prone to blundering every now and then. We gravitate to leaders who understand that they're human, too—just like the rest of us.

*   *   *   *   *

Whether a leader leads an agency, manages a marketing department, consults to a team of architects, or teaches a cohort of physicians, by demonstrating *competence, caring, character,* and *consistency,* she is demonstrating her trustworthiness.

Like gratitude and so many other qualities of being, trust is a declaration of a leader's dependence—on his team members and other valued constituents. Trust is also a declaration of *inter*dependence. In other words, trust says, "If you give me something—your competence and gracious caring, your strong character and consistency—I'll give you something. I'll give you my respect, loyalty, and trust." This kind of interdependence is wonderfully demonstrated by my friend Helen.

Building Trust One Person at a Time

After her successful career as an attorney, Helen was not ready to retire. She wanted to serve in a new way. To equip herself for her encore career, she enrolled in a graduate program in social work. There she studied the beauty of living and dying, preparing for a career in hospice.

One afternoon, Helen shared her adventures with me over coffee. "Even though I loved my hospice studies, my favorite thing was to tutor students in the university's writing and research center. As I thought about how much I loved tutoring students, something clicked. I remembered my first love—teaching. After almost 40 years, I dusted off my K–12 teacher's certificate and applied for a substitute teacher position."

Connecting her values and her purpose, Helen is now teaching in a vibrant learning community. In the classroom, she is in her element. "I just love what I do. I feel like I'm in my own skin. From my very first day on the job, I felt at home." Within a few weeks, the district hired Helen as a full-time teacher.

Recently, we met again for coffee. Helen looked radiant as she shared her newfound excitement.

> When I'm in the classroom with my students, it's like I'm in a thriving garden. What promise and beauty! And what a privilege it is when I have a chance to tell my students what I see.

Smiling behind her steaming cappuccino, Helen recounts moments from her first few weeks as a substitute teacher.

> One day I gave my students an assignment to write a letter telling an employer why they were the right person for a job. "Think of your reliable strengths," I tell them. "What's natural and effortless for you that you can offer to others?"

> From the front row, an 8th grade girl blurts out, "What if you aren't good at anything?" As the rest of the class gets to work, I fix my attention on Sasha and kneel beside her chair.

> Looking into her big brown eyes, I tell her, "I've been watching you today. Every time I saw you, I felt warmth and relief to have you here. You are the best listener in the class."

Helen explains that because students are constantly told to listen, listening itself has become devalued in schools. Regrettably, only a few students master the art of listening; even fewer understand that listening is a responsibility and an art—a very special art. Indeed, it is a dance, an exquisite dance of communication…the turn of the head, the tracking of eyes, the opening of the heart.

> I confided to Sasha, "This skill—listening—will make you very valuable to others anywhere you apply it." Sasha tells me that she enjoys design and fabrics. I note the original way she has put her outfit together and acknowledge her talent.

> In just five minutes, another fragrant flower has bloomed in the garden.

> I tell you, every day I have to pinch myself to make sure I'm not dreaming….

Pointing out the many things she enjoys about substitute teaching, one of the most poignant is that it offers students an opportunity to make themselves new for a day. "They can try on a different persona or simply step more fully into, inhabit, and enjoy being in their own skin. Because they're not likely to see a substitute teacher again anytime soon and since the substitute teacher holds no power of academic evaluation over them, the students feel safe."

Delighted that students feel safe with her, Helen explains that students identified as "difficult" by their regular teacher often turn out to be the most responsive and eager learners.

> On the best days, they tell me their stories.

> They tell me the way you might tell a story to someone you meet only once—on a long bus ride perhaps. The first grader who wanted to die…so he could be with his grandpa. The quiet fifth-grade boy from Guatemala who misses his mother. When the family came north, she had to stay behind. The anxious

redhead who reported her mom had grown up seeing her mother being beaten by her father, the redhead's grandfather... who just moved in with them. The high school junior who has a job working with disabled children and knows that will be her life's work.

Into the embrace of a leader these intimate stories are given, stories that could only be surrendered in the gentle glow of competence, caring, and beneficial concern. Stories that are borne by the strong character—the lovely harbor of a trusted leader.

For any leader, building a sense of trust is a very high skill. To build trust as a substitute teacher is nothing short of remarkable. In a matter of a few hours, they must demonstrate *competence, caring, character*, and *consistency*. They must do so in a way that inspires and builds trust with their students. Clearly, as a substitute teacher, Helen ably established trust with her students. She accomplished this not because of her specific expertise or polished exterior. Her students trust her for her way of being. Because she has mastered the art of connecting who she is with what she knows and does, Helen continues to inspire trust in her role as a full-time teacher.

Flawless Leadership Practice

Practice being trustworthy.

Dr. Maya Angelou reminds us that "People will forget what you said, people will forget what you did, but people will never forget how you made them feel." Do you know how you make people feel?

Even though they may care deeply, sometimes leaders fall short on showing they care. Ask yourself: *Who do I really care about, but I haven't let them know?* This could be someone in your family or at work—a peer, a team member, or your boss.

Now...reflect for a moment. What is it about this person that causes you to care so deeply? If you can identify what you care about, you can unpack specific details. Nothing says caring like attending to the details. Not just hearing, but listening. Not just understanding, but empathy. Not just seeing, but peering into the quiet, hidden places. Caring is about intimacy. As a play on words, intimacy translates to in-to-me-see.

Leaders who can see into the qualities of others have the capacity to reflect them back. When we notice details and play them back to another person, we touch their heart. The perfect grace note, that's what demonstrating caring is all about.

Chapter 8

Be Courageous

Courage is not the absence of fear...it's learning to confront it and overcome it.

NELSON MANDELA

MORE THAN ANY OTHER QUALITY CONNECTED TO leadership, courage seems to inspire the broadest spectrum of responses.

For example, world-class athletes describe courage as being bold, daring, and audacious. Amateur and professional athletes sport shoes and shorts emblazoned with the names of corporate sponsors. Some of their symbols—such as Nike's "swoosh" logo and its famous "Just Do It" tagline—have become synonymous with courage.

Whether at the stadium or on the street, we see men and women wearing T-shirts and jerseys with memorable quotes about courage, such as: "Human beings are made up of flesh and blood, and a miracle fiber called courage." This quote is most often attributed to Olympic pentathlete and U.S. General George S. Patton. One of the world's most feared and renowned warriors, Patton also described courage as "fear holding on a minute longer."

Courage is not always epic or heroic, written in banner headlines across a sunlit sky. Sometimes courage is more like a candle, its warm light illuminating a corner where it's most needed. Perhaps this is the kind of courage that journalist Mignon McLaughlin writes about when she says, "The only courage that matters is the kind that gets you from one moment to the next."

Sentenced to life imprisonment for daring to resist South Africa's brutal apartheid laws, Nelson Mandela is often considered to be the epitome of courage. But this world statesman does not view himself as courageous. Nor does he view courage as innate. In fact, he asserts that no one is born courageous.

Indeed, for Mandela and the rest of us, courage is a choice. A choice we make daily. Sometimes several times a day.

The Courage to Lead

Courage comes from an old French word—*coeur*—which means heart. *Flawless leaders* choose to lead from their heart, embodying courage as a natural expression of who they are. Although this definition of courage is pretty straightforward, leading from their heart is anything but straightforward for some people.

Recently, I spoke with Peter, an executive at a large Silicon Valley company. I'd just finished teaching a session on *flawless leadership*, focusing on what it means and what it takes to be courageous, to lead from the heart.

Peter said, "They sure don't teach you this stuff in business school. I want to know more. I want to learn how to lead from my heart, but I don't know where to begin," he confided. "Can you help me?"

I asked Peter about his leadership journey thus far. I also asked about what kind of personal and professional development he'd undertaken. Then I suggested a few resources that would be helpful and discussed next steps. Recognizing the courage Peter demonstrated by his request for help, I said, "Your team is very lucky to have a leader like you."

"My motive is pretty selfish. I have four children, all girls. Someday my daughters will work in the organizations engineered by guys like me—all head, but no heart. I can do something about that, starting with me. I'm ready and I look forward to the next leg of my leadership journey."

"Well, your daughters must mean an awful lot to you. Someday I'm sure they will thank you, and your team at work will, too."

Leading from the heart calls forth the best that's within us. Seasoned leaders can benefit by engaging a trusted ally or coach. Seasoned and emerging leaders alike can benefit by simply engaging in new experiences.

The Courage to Serve

For the past few years, I've taught emerging leaders to prepare them for their service-learning trip in Ghana. Each year, I witness the leaders' excitement and anticipation about their upcoming learning adventure. For some, I also witness their apprehension since this is their first trip away from home, let alone to a continent 10,000 miles away. Upon their return, I'm always humbled and amazed when they share their powerful testimonies of personal growth and transformation.

While there, each leader is engaged in a service project, working alongside Ghanaian doctors, teachers, and community elders. They also study leadership, looking through the lens of identity development and spiritual formation. During the trip and in the months that follow, each person experiences a breakthrough in some sphere of their life.

I'm always moved by the stories they share when they return. I was particularly touched by Sumaya's story. A bright-eyed, soft-spoken woman in her early 20s, she had assisted medical staff in the village clinic. In her own words, Sumaya shared her courageous, life-changing experience.

> Ever since I was a little girl, my parents have encouraged me to become a doctor. However, I didn't believe that was God's plan for me. Maybe I was just being defiant.
>
> While working in the clinic, something happened that I never would have dreamed. During my first week, I helped deliver a baby. I was really scared and don't know how I did it, but I did. A few days later, I helped deliver another baby, then another. All told, I helped deliver seven babies!
>
> When I told my parents and friends what happened, they all said I sounded so excited. I *was* excited. I was also honored and profoundly changed. I really enjoyed helping each woman bring their child into the world. And I learned so much about caring for others…and for myself.
>
> Because of my incredible experiences while working in the clinic, I've decided to become a pediatrician. I now know this is God's plan for me.

Like many young people, particularly women, Sumaya suffered from low self-esteem. Unsure of herself and her strengths, she often felt as though she was simply drifting through life without direction or purpose. But through her work in the clinic in Ghana, her self-image shifted. Realizing that she could make a positive difference in others' lives, a difference that brought joy to them and her, Sumaya's self-worth blossomed.

Because of her experience in Ghana, Sumaya recognized that she had much to offer and a genuine desire to serve, and her awakening gave her a sense of direction and purpose she'd never experienced before. When she returned from Ghana emboldened with a new sense of courage, Sumaya immediately applied for and was accepted into a pre-med program. She has become an exemplar for other emerging leaders.

Be Audacious and Daring

Our times call for leaders at all levels. Not just positional leaders. Teams, organizations, and nations need people who will take a stand and speak up, regardless of their position, title, or rank. People who are self-aware and self-responsible. People with the courage to challenge an idea or a point of view—even when it is not popular to do so.

In any organization or community, there will always be opportunities for you to step up, take a stand, and demonstrate your courage in support of an idea, a cause, a person, or a group of people. The invitation is to demonstrate courage as a routine, everyday choice. This kind of courage separates *flawless leaders* from the wanna-bes—those leaders who *think* about stepping up, yet lack the courage to do so.

Flawless leaders know that living courageously has a positive impact on others. They know that how courageously they live their own life determines the extent to which the people around them will sense their own courage.

When we demonstrate courage, we actually *en*courage others. Igniting a spark within them, we give them a glimpse of what it means and what it looks like to live and lead from the heart. To live and lead with clarity about who they are, what they believe, and what they value. To venture into uncharted territory, leaving the familiar behind. With that encouragement, they can become non-positional leaders, ones who lead from their heart. These kinds of leaders work toward a common goal, offer their expertise, accept responsibility, and inspire others.

Positional leaders rely on these courageous souls. In fact, they seek out non-positional leaders to receive the gift of their support and collaboration. Positional leaders value non-positional leaders as mentors who can tell them what's working in the organization and what's broken. Positional leaders also value non-positional leaders as allies to advise them about who to rely on and who not to.

The truth is, we are all non-positional leaders in some aspect of our lives. As such, we all ignite, influence, and inspire others. We do it every day. When you speak, others listen. They hear and are affected by what you say. When you assist someone—or not—others see you. Their lives are affected, touched, and changed in some way. They discover something about you, and if they're lucky, they also discover something about themselves, sparked by your actions.

As you gain greater clarity about who you are and who and what you care about, being courageous will become easier. Let's face it, you don't have to be the CEO to be courageous. You don't even have to have a college degree to be courageous. You only need to speak and act from your heart—with caring and concern for others, buoyed by a servant heart.

Flawless Leadership Practice

Practice being courageous.

Think about a time in your life when you felt fearful or small. Let yourself slip back to that time. What was happening? Who was with you? How did you feel?

Now reimagine that moment. Instead of shrinking back in fear, stand tall. Plant your feet firmly on the floor, spread about a foot apart. Straighten your back and pull yourself up so that your shoulders are square, your spine is straight, and your neck is comfortable. Chin up and out. Hold your ground. Now take one step forward, then another. Walk tall.

How might walking tall, rather than playing small, have helped you in your leadership journey?

How might it help you now?

Even when you feel fearful and small, when you walk tall, you *en*courage yourself and invite courage in others. Sometimes, you actually ignite courage, arousing others' hearts in the midst of the storm.

PART IV

HOW WILL I CHANNEL MY PASSION TO SERVE OTHERS?

HOW WILL I LIVE MY LIFE?

The heart of the leader is manifested through service to others.

DR. ARTIKA R. TYNER

Chapter 9

Be a Dreamer

*Every great dream begins with a dreamer. Always remember
you have within you the strength, the patience, and the passion
to reach for the stars to change the world.*

ANONYMOUS

RECENTLY I READ *LEADERSHIP 2050*, a book that explores the future of
leadership. Curated and written by leaders, leadership developers,
and leadership educators, this group of diverse experts are dreamers.
Devoted visionaries and agents of change, these men and women
are keenly aware of where humanity would be without leaders who
delve into the fiery realm of dreams.

The essays in *Leadership 2050* project a world that will
be very different than the one we know. The authors consider a
constellation of forces most likely to influence and inspire leaders
and followers during the next 35 years.

So, what are the key challenges, contexts, drivers, and opportunities that will most likely shape the future of leadership? In this future, who will we recognize as leaders? Who must be welcomed to the table who is not there now?

Together We Can

While we can't predict the future, we can anticipate a world where wicked challenges will increase, a world where conventional approaches will no longer suffice and adaptive solutions will become the norm. Consequently, we can envision a future that not only privileges technology and science, but also prizes the subtle yet unmistakable wisdom of the human heart and soul. A future where non-traditional and non-positional leaders are valued for their unique sensibilities and contributions and are engaged beyond their traditional roles and boundaries.

Today's non-traditional and non-positional leaders include artists; young people; elders; girls and women; refugees; people who are poor, homeless, incarcerated, in gangs, trafficked, terrorized, or otherwise objectified and marginalized. If we are to co-create a just and humane future—a world that works for all—we must dream a world that welcomes and hosts all voices. To deny, mute, or omit some voices in favor of others' is to miss the opportunity to realize humanity's highest potential in the spheres of art, commerce, ecology, education, faith, government, science, technology, and beyond.

When people with diverse gifts, life circumstances, and worldviews dream together, they can spark imaginative and innovative breakthroughs—big and small. The great Irish poet Seamus Heaney said, "If you have the words, there's always a chance that you'll find the way." Similarly, if you have the right people in the conversation, there's always a chance they'll find a way. Create the right conditions with the right voices at the table, and the opaque will become clear. The strange familiar. The impractical practical.

Put Wings on Your Dreams

Dr. Johnnetta Cole is a dreamer. And she knows that a dream without a plan is merely a wish. Born into a family of high achievers, Cole's great-grandparents, grandparents, and parents were pillars in the African-American community. Her maternal great-grandfather, Abraham Lincoln Lewis, co-founded Florida's first insurance firm, a venture that years later would make him the state's first African-American millionaire.

Into this atmosphere, Johnnetta set her sights on achieving dreams of greatness. And she has done just that, not for herself but on behalf of her beloved country. As the first African-American president of Spelman College and in her early work as a professor, Dr. Cole dreamed of reimagining the racial narrative of the United States of America. She has relentlessly pursued her dream so that we, the American people, might live into our greatness and potential as a people and as a nation.

As an historian and as a custodian of the future, Dr. Cole calls us to a higher ground. "This," she says, "is a nation whose spoken and written vision is chillingly beautiful." Thus she summons us into the realm of desire and transcendence, a future realm where there is equity and justice for all.

Such is the beauty and power of dreams.

The Power of Commitment

Albert Einstein said, "Imagination is everything. It is the preview of life's coming attractions." That coming attraction is you, your advisory board, your cadre of community volunteers. That coming attraction is the marvelous work you will do together to bring your dreams to fruition.

Because they call us to live into our greatness, our dreams must be infused with imagination, shored up by faith, and undergirded by intention. Whether it's for you, your family, your organization, or your community, dreams must also be powered by the fuel of commitment.

Commitment activates forces and resources to support us in realizing our dreams. About the power and significance of commitment, Scottish mountaineer and writer W. H. Murray shares this reflection about his dream to join a Himalayan expedition to explore one of the world's most rugged and remote mountain ranges:

> But when I said nothing had been done, I erred in one important matter. We had definitely committed ourselves and were halfway out of our ruts. We had put down passage money— booked a sailing to Bombay. This may sound too simple, but it is a great consequence. Until one is committed, there is hesitancy, the chance to draw back, always ineffectiveness. Concerning all acts of initiative (and creation), there is one elementary truth the ignorance of which kills countless ideas and splendid plans: that the moment one definitely commits oneself then Providence moves too. A whole stream of events issues from the decision, raising in one's favor all manner of unforeseen incidents, meetings and material assistance, which no man [or woman] could have dreamt would come his way.

CEOs, city council members, and members of Congress know the hesitancy that Murray so eloquently describes. We all do. We also know the catalytic power of commitment.

Commitment commands. Understanding that all daring begins with a dream, Murray concludes by penning this about commitment: "Whatever you can do or dream you can do, begin it. Boldness has genius, power, and magic in it."

Commitment asserts, "We know what we want. And nothing, absolutely nothing will stop us until we achieve it." Why? Commitment blasts through barriers. And because commitment knows that anything worth doing can't be accomplished alone, it welcomes support. Indeed, commitment turns blueprints into buildings…hopes into hip-hop beats…inspired ideas into innovative inventions and interventions.

Commitment turns vision into volition.

Discern and Clarify Your Vision

Where would our world be without those who dream? Dreamers are the architects, composers, gardeners, and magicians of the future. They are the bearers of light. They know that persons with vision shine a light into the overlooked, hidden, and forgotten places in their neighborhoods and organizations. They also understand that a vision is never static. It's alive. Dynamic and vibrant, a vision is a living entity that must be tended, nurtured, and re-visited to ensure that it remains relevant and "evergreen."

Whether you are creating a new vision or re-visiting an existing one, use these questions to discern and clarify your vision:

Where am I right now? Beginning right where you are provides a clear picture of reality. Your current reality is called HERE.

Where do I want to be? Knowing where you want to be provides direction. Where you want to be is called THERE.

What must I do to get from HERE to THERE? Clarifying your reality and where you want to be helps you identify your goals, priorities, and action steps—your GPS for short.

Once you get a clear view of where you are, where you want to go, and identify the GPS that will get you from HERE to THERE, ask yourself these questions:

How will my team, agency, organization, or community be different because of my choices—a month from now? A year from now? In 3 years? Identifying what will be different helps you visualize and internalize the impact you can expect.

Because of my choices, what three things will be improved for my team, my parish, or my university? Understanding what will improve helps you understand the value you will add.

To begin, what one step will I commit to today? Choosing one step that you will begin today puts your plan in motion.

It takes only one step to start a process. Once the process starts, other forces will be unleashed to support you in achieving your goals and realizing your vision.

In addition to helping you clarify your own vision, these questions will also help you envision or reimagine the team or organization entrusted to you. When creating a vision for your group, team, or organization, be sure to include them. If you don't, there will be no ownership. If there's no ownership, there will be no commitment. If there's no commitment, even the best vision will languish and eventually die.

Follow Your Vision, Not Someone Else's

There's a world of difference between having a vision that propels you to achieve it and pulling an idea out of thin air that has no connection to who you are and the skills you have. That's why it is essential to:

Be in harmony with your purpose. This means being attuned, which is all about continuously developing your self-awareness and self-knowledge. As we grow and develop in our awareness, we have access to a more expansive view of our purpose.

Connect your vision to who you are, why you're here, and what you care about. When we begin to act on our vision, it is important that we are vitally connected to it. Because when we are, we're pulled towards it, and where others see obstacles and barriers, we'll see just another leg of our journey.

Each day, take a step towards your vision. This is the only way to achieve your vision, to bring your hopes and desires into fruition. My dad used to tell me, "A dream won't work unless you do." In other words, dreams don't just happen. They are made. Dreams manifest into concrete form only through our intention and our effort.

Turn your vision into a plan: be intentional. Unpack your vision to grasp what will be required to accomplish it. As you gain more clarity, you will turn your vision into concrete goals, creating a plan of action for you to follow. Your plan can be written or visual—whatever works best for you.

Act on your plan. Doing so puts fuel in your car. When you put your foot on the pedal, the car will take you where you want to go…and to the next place and the next place after that.

Remember, following the path to your vision is a process, and each step is iterative. As you develop and grow, revisit each of these steps to ensure you are attuned and growing into your highest and fullest potential.

Whether your focus is yourself, your family, your team, or your organization, the process is the same.

Make Each Day a Masterpiece

There are three types of people in the world. There are people who *watch* things happen. There are people who *make* things happen. There are people who ask, *What happened?!*

What kind of person are you?

I'm certainly not the kind of person to sit back and watch things happen. Are you? Of course not. If you've read this far, like me, you are the kind of person who dares to make things happen. But being someone who makes things happen doesn't occur by accident. It happens by design, even if the design isn't readily apparent.

When I was a little girl, my mom would often say, "Tomorrow isn't promised." Back then, I didn't fully understand what she meant. But I now understand that my mom was really saying, *Today is a gift. Make it count. Make something happen.* Then and now, my mom's wise counsel spurs me on.

One of the most exciting days in my life was the day I realized that I was living from my life's dream, my life's purpose. That was the day I also realized that life is not a rehearsal. It was up to me to make my life count. No one else was going to do that for me. Since that day, I committed to make every day count. To make each day a masterpiece.

*   *   *   *   *

The future belongs to those who dream—and to those who prepare for it today. Truly, if we can imagine our future, we can shape it. If we can shape the future, we can also transform it. As women, men, and young people of vision and leadership, we offer the marvelous symphony of our lives as we dare to dream, reach for the stars, and transform the world.

Flawless Leadership Practice

Practice being a dreamer.

Ask yourself: *What will I do to make my life a masterpiece?* Or, *What will I do to make my team or classroom a masterpiece?* Or, *What will I do to make my council, my alliance, my country a masterpiece?*

If these questions seem like big questions, you're right. They are. Whenever I get in over my head, which is often, I simply remember that wonderful Wisdom Saying—*The journey of a thousand miles begins with one step.*

So, what step will you take today?

Chapter **10**

Be Inspired

When we are reaching for inspiration, we do well to reach first for humility.

Julia Cameron

Like moths that are drawn to a flame, we're naturally drawn to people who inspire us. We also want our leaders to be inspiring. But before leaders, or anyone for that matter, can inspire others, they first must *be* inspired.

Inspire comes from *inspirare*, which means to breathe into or upon. To become inspired, we must be infused with life from a force outside of ourselves.

How does this happen?

Inspiration Begins with Humility

Unfortunately, too many leaders focus on themselves. Leading from their ego, they act on their need to be seen as superior in some way. When leaders act purely on their need to be seen, this is a recipe for disappointment and disaster. Such leaders are neither inspired or inspiring.

Flawless leaders are humble, gathering inspiration by asking *Who can I serve today? How can I be of use?* And they wait, allowing that gentle infusion of a whispered response. Only then are they moved to action.

Leaders who focus on serving first find that their lives are more fluid. Relationship snags clear up. Drama decreases or disappears. They speak to others not from their head but from their heart, from a place of genuine caring and concern. They are motivated by kindness, mercy, and generosity. Moving from a center of gratitude and authenticity, such leaders ask, *What can I do for you?* Rather than feeling constrained or constricted, these leaders feel a sense of expansion, liberation, and possibility.

Surrendering to the Flow

In her lovely book *Finding Water*, artist and writer Julia Cameron teaches that inspiration is our "willingness to surrender to a higher octave, the finer vibration that the work itself might hold." *Flawless leaders* are inspired because they know how to surrender. They know how to let go.

Artists describe this kind of surrender as being in a state of flow. In this place we become the channel for something that wants to move through us. About his beautiful operatic masterpiece *Madame Butterfly*, composer Giacomo Puccini said, "The music of this opera was dictated to me by God. I was merely instrumental in putting it on paper and communicating it to the public."

As painter and poet, scientist and sculptor, Michelangelo also understood what it was to be a channel, and to surrender as an instrument of the Divine. Remarking about his exquisite sculpture of *David*, he reveals, "I saw the angel in the marble and carved until I set him free."

On a recent trip to Tuscany, I had the good fortune to once again witness Michelangelo's artistry. Standing at the foot of his magnificent sculpture of *David*, I was transported to another realm. There I recognized that the artist's and the leader's task is one and the same: to release our resistance, to simply surrender to what wants to be born through us *and* our organizations.

Shifting Our Perspective

A change in scenery can yield renewed inspiration. Because it shifts our perspective, we return to our normal routine and relationships with fresh eyes and new insights. To change our scenery, we can take a walk, read a book, travel to another city or country, ride our bike to work, watch a great movie, garden, golf, or go fishing. I love music. Certain kinds of music help me shift my perspective, putting me in a whole new frame of mind. Music also helps me learn the rhythm of new cultures—literally and metaphorically.

As the face of leadership and the faces of leaders continue to change, learning the rhythm of new cultures will become a prized asset, a way of being, a way of life. Leaders need fresh perspectives. Leaders acting from outmoded frames of reference will flounder, and even fail. And a leader who acts alone or in isolation will face far greater perils than her counterpart who understands the importance of igniting the inspired wisdom of the many.

But how? Perhaps by shifting our perspective and, when needed, by shifting our paradigm.

Many years ago, one of my mentors asked if I'd ever visited Africa. At that time, I'd only dreamed about such a journey.

"Why do you ask?" I responded.

"When you do, your work will be different."

"How so?"

"Your soul will be transformed."

Years later, when I visited Africa for the first time, I came to fully understand and live into my mentor's prescient words. As the Boeing 747 descended through the bright blush of Kenya's equatorial sunrise, vast expanses of land came into view at a scale humans could comprehend. During our approach to Nairobi, I surveyed mile after mile of rust-red earth flanked by voluptuous green hills. As the plane continued its descent, I noticed that many of the hillsides were terraced beneath a heavy overgrowth of vines.

Just as the wheels of the plane touched the runway, I felt a burst of energy course through my entire body. Unlike the typical jolt one experiences when a jetliner touches down, mine was the shock of recognition and deep remembrance. The shock of my body awakening to what my soul already knew.

The specter of red clay dirt and vine-shrouded hills was not unlike the terrain of my childhood home in rural Mississippi— some 10,000 miles across the Atlantic. Little did I know that this landscape of red roads and green hills would be the first of many instances of my soul remembering my motherland of Africa.

During my month-long stay in Kenya, I discovered the origins of what I'd known and experienced all my life, beginning in Mississippi. There my experience had a name: community. In Kenya and in many other parts of Africa, community had another name—*Ubuntu* (pronounced ooo-BOON-too).

My perspective had shifted, and I was inspired!

Learn from the Spirit of *Ubuntu*

Although most Westerners are unfamiliar with the term *Ubuntu*, we are actually quite familiar with many of its aspects. Years ago, a friend sent me a Christmas card, which I saved because I love the inspirational greeting. I keep it on my writing table. On a wintry background, illuminated red letters proclaim the spirit of Christmas, giving us a glimmer, a small yet significant glimpse into the heart and spirit of *Ubuntu*.

❋ The SPIRIT of Christmas is found anytime that PEOPLE add BEAUTY to living. ❋ By thinking of OTHERS and showing they CARE, ❋ by HELPING and TRUSTING and GIVING. ❋ It's found anytime someone's DREAM becomes real by the KINDNESS another extends. ❋ The SPIRIT of Christmas is found ALL YEAR through in the SPIRIT of LOVE between FRIENDS. ❋

In the lovely, inspirational book *Believe*, Archbishop Emeritus Desmond Tutu defines *Ubuntu*. Read the honorable archbishop's words and notice what's already familiar to you about *Ubuntu*:

> The definition of this concept has two parts. The first is that the person is friendly, hospitable, generous, gentle, caring, and compassionate. In other words, someone who will use his or her strengths on behalf of others—the weak and the poor and the ill—and not take advantage of anyone. This person treats others as he or she would be treated. And because of this, they express the second part of the concept, which concerns openness, large-heartedness. They share their worth. In doing so my humanity is recognized and becomes inextricably bound to theirs.

Providing contextual dimension to this way of being, living, and moving through the world, Archbishop Tutu elaborates:

> People with *Ubuntu* are approachable and welcoming; their attitude is kindly and well-disposed; they are not threatened by the goodness in others because their own esteem and self-worth is generated by knowing they belong to a greater whole. To recast the Cartesian proposition, "I think, therefore I am," *Ubuntu* would say, "I am human because I belong." Put another way, a person is a person through other people, a concept captured by the phrase "me we."

In my travels to various parts of Africa, I have experienced many people with *Ubuntu*. One of my dear friends and traveling companions has traveled to many more countries in Africa than I have, and her experiences echo mine. Recently, she sent me this lovely story that delves deeper into the heart of *Ubuntu*.

> An anthropologist studying the habits and customs of an African tribe found himself surrounded by children most days. So, he decided to play a little game with them. He managed to get candy from the nearest town and put it all in a decorated basket at the foot of a tree. Then he called the children and suggested they play the game. When the anthropologist said "Now," the children had to run to the tree. He told them that the first one to get there could have all the candy for him or herself.
>
> So the children all lined up waiting for the signal. When the anthropologist said "Now," the children took each other by the hand and together they ran towards the tree. They all arrived at the same time, divided up the candy, sat down, and began to happily munch away.
>
> The anthropologist went over to them and asked why they had all run together when any one of them could have had all the candy to themselves. The children responded: "*Ubuntu*. How could any one of us be happy if all the others were sad?"

Clearly, *Ubuntu* is not only a quality, it is also a way of being, a way of living. Epitomized by a marvelous worldview, *Ubuntu* is the essence of what it means to be human. Indeed, in some African cultures, to acknowledge and appreciate someone for their *Ubuntu* nature is regarded as the highest praise.

What I learned about *Ubuntu* in Kenya and elsewhere in Africa echoed and reaffirmed what I already knew about aboriginal and indigenous cultures, including African, American, Australian, Chinese and the many cultures that emerged from China, Maori, and Pacific Islanders. Called by different names in these diverse cultures, the cultural inflections of *Ubuntu* are similar to what many Westerners variously refer to as servant-leadership. By any name, it is inspired and calls us to live and lead in a way that is at once focused on both the collective and the individual.

Flawless Leadership Practice

Practice being inspired.

See yourself in a whole new light.

Set aside an hour once a week or once a month to learn more about the richness of your own culture.

Begin by asking yourself: *What country or town or village did my family come from? What did they enjoy doing? What did they accomplish? What hardships did they face?*

Let your heightened awareness and knowledge of what you learn about your ancestry inform, transform, and inspire you.

Now, ask yourself: *What do I know about my grandmother or grandfather? My great-grandmother and great-grandfather? Were they olive farmers or merchants in Italy, Israel, or Greece? Were they sheepherders in Ireland or France? Tradesmen in Tibet? Could they have been cheesemakers or cobblers in Denmark, chieftains or cotton weavers in Mali or Nigeria?*

Whoever they were, whatever they did, your relatives had dreams and aspirations, just like you. They danced, loved, prayed, and sang. They understood the power of community—in the family, in the marketplace or town square, in the church or mosque, on village roads, in the huts or halls of government.

Ask yourself: *How might what I learn about my family inspire me? How might my learning breathe new life into my leadership? Into how I work with my team? Into how I contribute to my community?*

Chapter **11**

Be a Learner

*Then let us all do what is right, strive
with all our might toward the unattainable,
develop as fully as we can the gifts God has given us,
and never stop learning.*

LUDWIG VON BEETHOVEN

WE LIVE IN AN AGE WHERE KNOWLEDGE IS MORE easily accessible
for the masses than ever, so why do we now believe learning is
on the decline? One of the main reasons is because we've shifted
the focus in how we educate our children. We prime students to
begin preparing for specific jobs in middle school and sometimes
earlier. Furthermore, our colleges and universities have become
increasingly focused on preparing students for specific professions
rather than on teaching them how to learn.

Teaching a person to be an accountant or an analyst, an
engineer or an economist, a project manager or a programmer is
far different than teaching them how to be a learner. Too often we

prepare persons for a job or career who become professionals with mediocre minds. We prepare them to become expert problem-solvers perhaps, but they do not understand how to adapt their approaches or methods of problem-solving. In other words, they become learned, but they simply don't know how to be a learner.

What Does It Mean to Be a Learner?

In his poem "A Learned to Learner Litany of Transformation," Leonard Sweet captures the world of difference between merely being learned and what it means to be a learner.

> When I was learned, knowledge went to my head. Now that I'm a learner, knowledge travels the longest foot in the universe—the foot that separates my head from my heart.

> When I was learned, I looked to the past: to have confirmed the set of beliefs I already had. Now that I'm a learner, I look to the future: to grow, be stretched, and remain open to what I don't know.

If you're like most people, you will resonate with being learned. After all, that's how most of us are formed. From the time we're born and throughout our formative years, there's someone hovering over us, instructing us: "Do *this*, not *that*. Do it *this* way, not *that* way. Do it *my* way, not *your* way. When *I* talk, *you* listen. *Don't* talk back." Over time, we internalize these commands. We become learned. And if we're not careful, we can become hardened, calcified, unchangeable.

Social philosopher and author Eric Hoffer says, "In times of change, learners inherit the earth, while the learned find themselves beautifully equipped to deal with a world that no longer exists." I don't know about you, but being a learner certainly sounds more exciting to me!

So what does it mean to be a learner? Learners love to learn. In fact, they are passionate about learning, and they view it as a life-long adventure. They relish learning about anything and everything. However, learners don't merely learn for the sake of learning. They do so to integrate learning as a way of being.

Like *flawless leaders*, learners look to the future. They view learning as an open invitation to serve, grow, and even unlearn in order to learn anew. As such, they will be equipped to live and lead in the world as it is emerging, to live and lead on the frontier.

Learning Is an Act of Service

Flawless leaders learn so they can serve others. They know that if they want to serve others well, they must continuously sow into, invest in, and develop themselves. Why? Leaders can't give what they don't have. Nor can they take others to places they have never been.

Leaders who continuously invest in their own learning and growth understand that this is the greatest gift they can give to others. As they continuously invest in their own development and growth, these leaders will come to understand that their life is not their own. They will come to know that their life belongs to others.

Understanding that his was a life of service, playwright and Nobel Laureate George Bernard Shaw said, "I am of the opinion that my life belongs to the whole community, and as long as I live, it is my privilege to do for it whatever I can." So complete was Shaw's commitment to serving others, he declared:

> I want to be thoroughly used up when I die, for the harder I work the more I live. I rejoice in life for its own sake. Life is no brief candle to me. It is a sort of splendid torch which I have got hold of for the moment, and I want to make it burn as brightly as possible before handing it on to the future generations.

Because they are in it for the long haul, *flawless leaders* cultivate the habit of life-long learning. They fully understand that they learn *so that* they benefit this generation and the generations to come.

Learning Is About Growth

As an educator and former corporate leader, I've witnessed all kinds of learners. Some learners are adventurous; daring diggers, they love unearthing the new. Some are tenacious observers who pay careful attention to the people and events around them. Some are grazers who love to nibble on a few juicy nuggets, take a break, then enthusiastically come back for more. All are curious, open, eager, and engaged.

The best learners understand two things that elude others. They recognize that learning is imperative in order to grow and that if they're not growing, they're actually withering, shrinking, and dying on the vine. Secondly, these learners realize that they facilitate their growth by stepping back, reflecting on, and evaluating what they're learning. In your quest for learning, reflection gives you an opportunity to examine what you're consuming. Then evaluation allows you to critique your experience. If you're not reflecting and evaluating, you're just going through the motions. But you're not learning.

Being a learner means being intentional about learning something new every single day—anytime, anywhere, and with anyone. I refer to these people as 365/24/7 learners, because they simply learn from any and every situation and in every area of their life.

Learning Is About Unlearning

So they can be learners in the best sense, *flawless leaders* understand the benefit of unlearning rigid values, beliefs, and behaviors and learning new ones. They know that anything that can be learned can be unlearned.

In our effort to reimagine and remake our world into one that works for all, *flawless leaders* unearth and confront the lies many of us were taught as young people. For example, by now, most of us understand that race is a construct created by humans. Many of us cry or cry out for people who are destitute, who are homeless, who go hungry. But poverty is not accidental. Neither is homelessness and hunger. Along with slavery and apartheid, these constructions are made by human beings.

Here's the good news: what we construct can be deconstructed. We dismantle by our thoughtful, compassionate choices and actions. In other words, if we can learn something we can also unlearn it and substitute new learning in its place.

Learning While Crawling on the Floor with the CEO

Sometimes our lessons and what we learn from them come in surprising packages. What started as a conversation about values alignment ended with me and my client Rhea crawling around on her office floor. Wielding crayons and markers, we were like two little kids as we excitedly mapped out the future trajectory of her organization.

Let me explain.

Each year I review my roster of clients to ensure that we're still a good fit for each other in terms of our values and priorities. Seated in comfortable, overstuffed chairs, I proceed to tell my client Rhea that my values and priorities and those of her organization no longer align. "Given your organization's expertise and financial assets, you are uniquely positioned to have a much broader reach and impact. But you seem content to operate from your comfort zone rather than your stretch zone. Rhea, as much as I enjoy working with you and your team, it seems to me that you don't need my services anymore."

After a few beats, Rhea politely thanks me for my candid observations and shares how much she enjoys working with me. "Is there anything else?"

I'm still seated, but mentally I'm already out the door. "No."

"Well," she says, "if you're interested, I'd like to share what I have up my sleeve."

My interest piqued, I stay put.

As Rhea lays out the vision for her organization, I listen with the ears of a deer. When she's done, I blurt, "Now, I would love to be part of *that* vision. May I share some of my thoughts with you?"

That's when Rhea called her assistant to bring in the crayons, markers, and paper.

As we created the 20-year vision for her organization, I learned a lot from my client. And I learned a lot about myself: learning is about taking risks, being vulnerable, staying centered, suspending judgment, paying attention, experimenting, enabling others, and being curious.

Learning Through Play

Flawless leaders are relentless learners. They easily learn from any circumstance and in any context, just like my client Omar who shared this story.

> One summer afternoon, I was on the beach with my son. While I worked, he and his friend were busy building a sandcastle near the shore. Next to me, his bottle of bubbles was wedged in the sand. Noodling about a problem I faced with my project team, I idly opened the lid and lifted the plastic wand filled with soapy water.
>
> I really don't know how long I wrestled with the problem in my head, but I was jarred from my thoughts when my son yelled, "Daddy, Daddy, come, look at our castle." I jogged down to the water's edge with the wand still in my hand, holding it high into the wind.

As Omar ran, the wind gently pushed the soapy water through the little wand, transforming the pearly liquid into a stream of beautiful bubbles. Watching the bubbles escape from the wand, his smile turned into laughter as he marveled at a simple miracle.

> When the bubbles broke free, the problem I'd been wrestling with loosened its grip. In that instant, I realized this problem wasn't mine to solve. I also realized that I was caught up in one of my familiar patterns—overfunctioning.

As a classic overfunctioner myself, I could certainly relate. Omar and I enjoyed a good laugh, then he shared this reflection.

> If I had continued to think about the problem as mine, I would have done what I usually do—create confusion and chaos in my team…and I would have robbed them of an opportunity to use their own problem-solving abilities.

Learning from Other Cultures

It's been said that the difference between managers and leaders is that managers do things right and leaders do the right things. But what if leading is even more expansive than *doing* the right things? What if leading is about *being* fully present? About *being* open to hosting the talents and gifts of others?

I particularly enjoy learning about and from our sisters and brothers from cultures different than our own. Fortunately, my work takes me to different places around the world, so I can do just that. A few years ago, I was in Sydney, Australia to give a presentation. Honored as one of their top presenters, I was then invited back the next year by the conference organizers. To my delight, they asked me to deliver the closing keynote.

That next year, I presented on how to take your leadership to a whole new level. I addressed leaders who were committed to making a difference in their own and others' lives, leaders who wanted to make the shift from success to significance. Rather than focusing on knowing or doing, I focused on being and becoming. In fact, I addressed many of the themes I cover in this book. Afterwards, I spoke with a number of people in the audience, including a person who introduced himself as Graham.

After we chatted for a while, he asked, "Are you Maori?"

"Not to my knowledge. Why do you ask?"

"What you spoke about today, my people, the Maori, have practiced for thousands of years. All the things you discussed so beautifully—gratitude, authenticity, integrity, faithfulness, being of service...my people refer to these values and practices as legacy."

Boom!

Once again, just as when my jumbo jetliner landed in Kenya, I felt a jolt of recognition and deep remembrance. The myriad events and experiences in my life led to and converged in my conversation with Graham. From this gentle man, I learned anew about the deep, abiding kinship among peoples and across cultures. I also became consciously aware of a new way to think about the qualities of being that nurture and sustain us in living and leading with ethical and moral intelligence...the qualities that give us the graciousness to live and lead on behalf of this generation and the generations to come...a quality of being that I call *legacy consciousness*.

Wherever you are, Graham...thank you for prompting and enabling my learning.

Flawless Leadership **Practice**

Practice being a learner.

When Omar picked up the wand from his son's bottle of bubbles, play became his ally.

Has play been an ally for you? In what way? What were

you doing? Who was with you? How did you feel? What did you learn? Be specific.

Have you incorporated what you learned from your play into your leadership?

If not, how might you adopt or adapt what you learned for your team or organization? Make a list of three or four things. Choose one and begin. Have fun. Experiment. Notice what happens. Experiment some more. Adapt, as needed.

Choose something else from your list. Begin again. Have fun. Experiment. Notice what happens. Notice what you are learning. Also, notice how you are being transformed through play. Experiment. Adopt. Adapt. Experiment some more.

Keep playing!

And…keep learning.

Chapter 12

Be Persevering

Perseverance is not a long race; it is many short races,
one after the other.

WALTER ELLIOT

ALTHOUGH HUMANITY IS ON AN ACCELERATED path of continuous change and upheaval, we can find solace in the fact that we know what it means and what it takes to persevere. We can find solace because we've done it before. Not once. Not twice. But over and over and over again.

We've struggled with diasporas and dislocation of people all over the world; we've confronted and counteracted unwarranted aggression in Bosnia, Liberia, and remote Himalayan hamlets; we've taken on the insidious destruction of the Great Barrier Reef off the coast of Australia and the mighty rainforests of the Amazon. We're also learning how to respect and welcome the wisdom of families, communities, and nations to solve their own challenges: instead of seeing them as victims to be rescued, we see their brilliant resourcefulness and honor their rights.

Whether in pursuit of a distant goal, surmounting incredible odds, or overcoming adversity, for those who have persevered, what particular qualities do they possess? Conviction, determination, discipline, persistence, tenacity, and grit. Yes. And they also embrace the quieter but no less vital qualities of humility, faith, forgiveness, patience, and gratitude.

Perseverance embraces all of these qualities and more.

For *flawless leaders*, the hallmarks of perseverance also include refusal and diligence. Refusal to accept the status quo, and uncommon diligence in the face of discouragement and extreme adversity. In other words, these leaders simply refuse to accept circumstances as given, and they are resolute in their determination to find a way over, under, around, or through.

Don't Ask Why, Ask: *Why Not?*

As leaders confront the daunting challenges of thriving in today's ever-changing world, it helps to remember that throughout the millennia human beings have vigorously persisted *and* persevered. It also helps to know that we stand on many broad shoulders. And that we're really no different than the millions of women and men who came before us. We're not the first and we certainly won't be the last to confront the challenges of adapting to survive.

Through the ages, families, tribes, and entire nations have persevered not only by asking why, but also by asking why not. And just like playwright Samuel Beckett's bewildered characters who are utterly convinced that they can't go on but do in fact go on, human beings are adept at finding ways to keep on keeping on. Not only do we find ways to persevere, we find ways to thrive and, ultimately, to flourish.

Relentless: Lessons from History

History provides numerous and diverse examples of those who persevered. Those who had a dream, who kept their eyes trained on the prize, who made necessary adjustments along the way. Those who refused to take "no" for an answer. Those who saw failure as merely another opportunity to course correct and try again. Those who transmuted *Impossible* to *I'm possible*. Those who were ignited by the fire of passion and purpose, driven by the fuel of commitment.

> The Wright Brothers achieved the first powered, pilot-controlled, sustained airplane flight, accomplishing a feat that for centuries many others had dreamed about, attempted, and failed to achieve. Persevering learners, these brothers owned a successful bicycle business before they became aeronautical pioneers. Not only did Wilbur and Orville Wright transport us into the skies and the Age of Flight, through their vision and tenacity they also ushered our world into the Age of Possibility.

> Ernest Shackleton, in his bold quest to be the first to cross Antarctica on foot, led his crew of 27 men from certain death. Just 85 miles from the glacier-laden continent, his ship became hopelessly trapped by unusually thick ice and was eventually crushed and destroyed. Bound together by an enduring vision of survival, respect, mutual cooperation, and beneficial sacrifice, these men survived the extreme, frozen wilderness for 24 months. Under his brave leadership and impeccable navigation, Shackleton and all of his men survived.

> Helen Keller at 18 months old was debilitated by an illness that rendered her blind, deaf, and mute. Under the tutelage of her devoted mentor and teacher Anne Sullivan, Keller circumvented what could have been a life of abject torture. With Sullivan's nurturing and Keller's quick mind and fierce determination, she soon mastered sign language and

Braille, and learned to read and write. A tireless advocate for persons with disabilities, Keller also became a prolific writer. Her autobiography, written over a century ago, is still in print and has been translated into 50 languages.

Leymah Gbowee dreamed of a better life for herself and her children. As a single-parent and refugee from Liberia, she had experienced the terrors of war, including sexual violence. Bearing witness to the worst of humanity, Gbowee helped lift Liberia out of a very dark period. To end their long war and stop the brutal violence and war against women in Liberia, she mobilized and organized women across ethnic and religious divides. Now, as an activist and ambassador for peace and justice for girls and women, Gbowee is a powerful leader whose calling is to raise up other female leaders. Along with her friend and President of Liberia Ellen Johnson Sirleaf, Gbowee won the Nobel Peace Prize.

Eunice Kennedy Shriver launched a small summer camp for young people with intellectual disabilities. During this time in our nation's history, people with intellectual disabilities were often institutionalized, not unlike Eunice's older sister Rosemary. Driven by her unwavering belief in the dignity and worth of every person, Eunice started Camp Shriver at her home near Washington, D.C. From this modest beginning, the Special Olympics was born. In 1968, the first international Special Olympics was held. Now, every day of the year a Special Olympics competition occurs in at least one of the 170 countries that host a local, regional, or national event. Shriver's visionary, influential, and courageous leadership transformed how the world sees, accepts, includes, and celebrates people with intellectual disabilities.

Dr. Wangari Maathai inspired the planting of 30 million trees in Kenya. She was hounded, viciously attacked, and imprisoned for teaching women in her homeland not only to plant trees to restore the devastated ecosystem, but to believe in and support democratic rights. Despite the many cultural, social, and political obstacles she faced, Maathai ultimately triumphed. Not only did she become the first African woman to win the Nobel Peace Prize for her contributions to sustainable development, democracy, and peace, she is now revered as the Mother of the Green Belt Movement, which has contributed to the planting of tens of millions of trees in African countries and many other countries throughout the world.

George Frederick Handel was dissuaded by his father from studying music. Fortunately, Handel's mother encouraged her young son to pursue music, even conspiring with him to practice "on the sly." Taken in by a prominent court composer, Handel mastered instrumental composition by the time he was 10 years old and vocal composition by his mid-20s. In the final decades of his life under the duress of extreme poverty, depression, and crippling illness, he composed *Messiah*. One of the most-loved musical masterpieces in the world, Handel completed his most renowned work in just 27 days.

Steve Jobs launched Apple when mainframe computer giants such as IBM and DEC still dominated the industry. Against seemingly impossible odds, Jobs eventually won over skeptical critics and consumers, growing Apple from a diminutive startup in the desktop computer market to become a mighty, formidable giant in the world of electronics. In 2014, Apple became the first U.S. company to be valued at $700 billion and is now the world's second largest technology company. Jobs' tempestuous spirit and persevering leadership made Apple's brand synonymous with extraordinary—in terms of innovation and customer delight.

Winston Churchill ascended to Great Britain's highest seat of power at the precise moment in history when his qualities of strategic, tenacious leadership were needed most. From his service as a soldier and military leader, he knew the dangerous drag of defeatism, to which his resolve and robust optimism served as the perfect counterpoint. World statesman and leader, Churchill is known as "the lion who roared," for when the British Empire needed him most, he stood against the nihilism of the Nazi forces. How very different Europe and the rest of our world would be without Churchill's keen intuition, dogged determination, and inspired leadership.

These stories and vignettes about perseverance provide numerous lessons. They provide lessons about vision, passion, commitment, effort, dedication, grace, focus, strength of character, collaboration, cooperation, building on the work of others, learning, fortitude, resilience, and optimism. All of these lessons are about qualities of being, qualities that are available to anyone.

What other lessons did you discover about perseverance— particularly about refusal to accept the status quo and diligence in the face of discouragement and extreme adversity?

One Leader's Journey to Hell and Back

Often those closest to us show us what it means and what it takes to persevere. Although the world will never know their names, we know who they are. The women, men, and children who know the sting of rejection, the blight of bigotry, the hurdles of dealing with poor health, the challenges of regaining their financial footing. The people who know that when life knocks you down, you can get back up…and begin again. And again…and again.

Gretchen knows what it means and what it takes to persevere and to begin again. I first met her several years ago in one of my workshops. Later, she completed another one of my workshops as well as an intensive program focused on leading from the inside out. With Gretchen's permission, I share her story, beginning with where she is now on her long journey to hell and back.

I'm currently enrolled in a graduate program in transformational leadership. During my studies, I've come to understand that passion combined with service equals leadership.

When I complete my program, I plan to serve women and children who are impacted by mental illness. As a leader dedicated to serving the needs of my community, I hope and pray that God will continue to bless me with opportunities to humbly support and heal others....

Eleven years ago, I found myself spiraling down from a nine-month roller coaster ride. During those months, I fluctuated between bouts of mania and major depression. While in a manic episode, I became psychotic and delusional. I literally thought myself to be the Queen of Sheba. In full African regalia, I crossed busy streets and extended my arms out to my sides with utter confidence that drivers would stop—just for me.

One day, convinced that a palace had been prepared for me and my two young sons, I proceeded to haul everything out of our house. In a state of unbridled energy and without warning, I dismantled our home and took nearly all of our belongings to Goodwill. My sons looked on with disbelief and terror.

Shortly after this episode, Gretchen became severely depressed and attempted suicide. Later, when she learned that she would lose custody of her sons, she was numbed into yet another state of depression and another attempted suicide. Months later, she found herself inside a tiny closet. As she leaned against the wall, the trail of destruction that had been following her spun before her eyes: Gretchen had lost her sons, her marriage, her family's belongings, her dignity, two jobs, and she was on the verge of being evicted. "The person who had experienced all these losses, trauma, and shame was not me."

Sobbing, Gretchen crumpled to her knees. As she felt her body hit the floor, she suddenly realized that something was deeply wrong. "I must be sick." Gretchen believes that her realization was heaven-sent. She could feel an invisible, benevolent hand lifting her up and out of hell.

After finally being diagnosed with bipolar disorder, Gretchen began her long, arduous journey of recovery. Although her losses have haunted and plagued her for many years, when she asked God why she'd gone through so much suffering, she began to experience a profound healing take hold in her spirit. As she was being healed, Gretchen begged God to show her how to handle her losses, turmoil, depression, and the abusive relationship that imprisoned her.

Gradually and gently God began to guide Gretchen to use her story to serve others. A wise and dedicated counselor suggested that she attend an "In Our Own Voice" (IOOV) presentation at a National Alliance on Mental Illness convention. Their presentation format consists of two people living with mental illness sharing their stories. "The moment they started to speak, I couldn't hold back my tears. In fact, I cried throughout the entire presentation, and I knew…I had found my venue."

Now a certified IOOV presenter, Gretchen is determined to help banish the stigma associated with mental illness and to bring hope and inspiration to those living with mental illness and those who are impacted by it. "Giving voice to my story has helped me to heal some of the pain, shame, insecurities, and guilt associated with living with bipolar disorder. It has also helped me discover my purpose."

While most of us will never go through the kind of ordeal that Gretchen endured, we can relate to her story because we've all experienced some kind of adversity or trauma in our own lives. Her story underscores that we can persevere, and we can begin again. More importantly, her story demonstrates that we can learn to be persevering from the circumstances of our daily lives and from the strength of our being—our inner selves.

This is particularly significant for leaders. The vast majority of leaders—positional and non-positional—learn to lead by and are rewarded for developing skills and competencies that are externally focused. Consequently, it doesn't even occur to them to draw on their internal resources—that rich aquifer of their inner being. Tapping into their being is literally outside of their paradigm of what it means and what it takes to lead.

Granted, most leaders will never share the vivid details of their personal story with anyone, let alone tell their story as their life's purpose. But let's face it, we share our stories all the time—365/24/7. How? We live our stories out loud through our daily choices and decisions. We live our stories by the company we keep, by the work we choose, by the books we read, by our conversations, by who we invite to our table—at home, at work, and in our community. Our personal story permeates how we live *and* how we lead.

Ultimately, when we share our stories—of trauma and tenacity, fortitude and fire, refusal and diligence—we shine a light for others. We shine a light for people whose names we may never know, helping them get from HERE to THERE.

Flawless Leadership **Practice**

Practice being persevering.

Consider your own journey in life. What struggles have you faced? What struggles did you overcome? What qualities of being did you draw on? What did you learn about yourself? What did you learn about perseverance?

Now…ask yourself: *As a leader, what have I refused—until now?* In other words, what do you see within yourself, your family, your team, your organization, your community, or your country that you want to change, improve, eliminate, reduce, or repurpose? For what purpose, process, product, or service?

Instead of settling—instead of merely accepting things as they are—change them. Choose something you really care about. Something you can commit to.

Start small. Ask yourself: *What can I do? What can I build on?* Consider obstacles you might face. Consider the resources you'll need—allies, champions, advocates, qualities of being, money, time, energy, equipment…a thought partner perhaps?

Start small. Take one step. Begin today.

Tomorrow, take another step. And again the day after that.

If you hit a snag, try again. If you stumble and fall, get up. Dust yourself off. Begin again. And again. And again.

Celebrate small victories. Then, keep going.

Keep on keeping on.

Chapter **13**

Be a Bridge Builder

*Our nation needs bridges, and bridges are built
by those who look to the future and dedicate themselves
to helping others. I don't know what the future holds,
but I know who holds the future: it is you.*

SANDRA DAY O'CONNER

ONE OF THE GREATEST GIFTS WE CAN GIVE is to be intentional about showing our care and concern for others. To express our love and appreciation. To build bridges for others who come after us.

I've been blessed to have many wonderful mentors in my life—"accidental" mentors and formal mentors. My accidental mentors include the wonderful children, women, and men who graced my life for only a brief moment, yet their impact was profound. Knowingly or unknowingly, they taught me valuable lessons about life and leadership. My formal mentors generously and graciously shared their hard-earned knowledge and pearls of wisdom over a period of months or years.

Accidental or formal, all my mentors built a bridge for me, helping me navigate life's tributaries without having to endure all of the same trials and difficulties they experienced. Have I encountered difficulties in my life? Of course. I've shared some of them with you in this book. Have I sometimes struggled as a leader? You bet! But here's what I know: I wouldn't be the person or leader I am today without the many bridges I've crossed, bridges built by kind, caring mentors.

Some of my mentors have walked with me. Some have sat with me in their office or home, offering me sage counsel, advice, and instruction. Others have sculpted, composed music, or written poems, inviting me into the imaginal realm of the arts so I could have the privilege of gleaning from their work whatever lessons I needed at the time. Some of my mentors were alive and well; I encountered others long after they were dead and buried. Such was the case with Will Allen Dromgoole who many years ago wrote a beautiful poem called "The Bridge Builder."

Build a Bridge for Others

When I first heard her poem, it spoke directly to my heart. Recently, I began to wonder where it came from and wanted to know more about the poet. Through my research, I learned that the poem first appears in Dromgoole's illustrated book *Rare Old Chums*, published in 1898. The author renders the poem in the form of a song called "Building the Bridge." It's sung by a young girl about her father, an elderly man who in near-darkness crosses a ravine filled with rushing water. When the man safely reaches the other side, rather than resuming his journey, he pauses to consider others: someone who might come upon the same ravine, but being less experienced might not make it safely to the other side.

Across the chasm, the daughter sees her kind-hearted father build a bridge, a span to spare others from the rising waters of a rushing tide. Through the eyes of his loving daughter, Dromgoole paints this heart-warming scene.

An old man going a lone highway,
Came, at the evening cold and gray,
To a chasm vast and deep and wide.
Through which was flowing a sullen tide
The old man crossed in the twilight dim,
The sullen stream had no fear for him;
But he turned when safe on the other side
And built a bridge to span the tide.

"Old man," said a fellow pilgrim near,
"You are wasting your strength with building here;
Your journey will end with the ending day,
You never again will pass this way;
You've crossed the chasm, deep and wide,
Why build this bridge at evening tide?"

The builder lifted his old gray head;
"Good friend, in the path I have come," he said,
"There followed after me to-day
A youth whose feet must pass this way.
This chasm that has been as naught to me
To that fair-haired youth may a pitfall be;
He, too, must cross in the twilight dim;
Good friend, I am building this bridge for him!"

What an arresting and poignant portrait of a leader! Often recited at retirement parties in praise of a leader's selflessness and service, "The Bridge Builder" should be read not only when leaders exit the scene. This poem should also be required reading for *incoming* leaders to instruct them in the fundamentals of both living and leading.

At the end of the day, leadership is about helping others get from HERE to THERE. Being a bridge builder is one of the best ways I know to do just that. How wonderful it is that you don't have to wait to build a bridge for others. You can begin right here, right now.

Make a Way Where There Is No Way

Being a bridge builder is also about making a way for others where there is, or seems to be, no way. Making a way for others is not only an action, it's also an attitude, a mindset, a worthy habit of the heart. *Flawless leaders* make a way for others by building bridges of all kinds: bridges that connect students, team members, or community members to various resources—people, projects, funding, and opportunities. Sometimes these waymakers even build bridges that connect us to ourselves.

On a recent visit to Paraguay, I was blessed to meet two amazing waymakers: Favio Chávez and Nicolás Gómez. Favio conceived, created, and now directs La Orquesta de Instrumentos Reciclados de Cateura, popularly known as the Landfill Harmonic Orchestra or Los Reciclados. Nicolás, or Colá, is a carpenter who now makes musical instruments for the orchestra.

Prior to creating this unusual ensemble, Favio was an environmental engineer. He worked at an enormous landfill adjacent to the community his pupils call home. Realizing that trash could be revitalized and given another purpose, Favio sought out Colá to salvage discarded oil cans, drain pipes, bottle caps, keys, and assorted utensils to fashion these items and other refuse into violins, violas, cellos, wind instruments, and more for the children to play. Thus began a journey and labor of love.

From its very humble beginnings in the tiny, close-knit community of Cateura, Los Reciclados now travels the world, sharing music and goodwill wherever they go. Indeed, the motto of this amazing musical ensemble is: *The world sends us its garbage, we send back music.*

But that's not all.

Before the landfill gave birth to the orchestra, the children of Cateura were destined to an intergenerational lifestyle of extreme poverty, a life where drug use is rampant and early teen pregnancy is the norm. With the orchestra, the girls and boys can now begin to envision a different way of life.

Favio and Colá hold the vision for a brighter future not only for the young people who are members of the orchestra, but also for their families and community. In fact, for these waymakers, the orchestra is just one pillar of a much bigger plan, a plan that includes assisting orchestra members with their scholastic work, supporting orchestra members in obtaining their first job by working on behalf of Los Reciclados, and providing better housing for the families. In this way, Favio and Colá are building a sturdy bridge that, when the musicians and their families walk on it, can transform their lives right here right now for this generation and for generations to come.

How Do You Make a Way?

So, how might you make a way for others? There are many ways. Here are just a few ideas that will help you cultivate a way-making attitude:

- Know that it's not about you.
- Remember the waymakers who helped you.
- Help others recognize their unique gifts and strengths.
- Support others in cultivating, amplifying, and leveraging their unique gifts and strengths.
- Encourage others to become life-long learners.
- Help others discover their purpose—their own North Star.
- Help and support others to live and lead from their purpose.

A leader who makes a way for others understands that in giving she is being a steward of the future, gratefully passing on gifts that were given to her. Chief among them is the gift of generosity.

When my family migrated from the South, we first moved to Detroit, Michigan and finally settled in Ann Arbor. There I met a woman who would change my life: Mary Jane Gillespie. If you've heard me speak or have read some of my other writings, perhaps you'll remember this story. I tell it again here because it's a pivotal story in my life. Not only did Ms. G. make a way for me, she built a bridge that saved my life.

Ms. G. was my sixth grade teacher. I became her student shortly after my family moved to Ann Arbor. In Detroit, most of my classmates and teachers were African-American. In my school in Ann Arbor, there were no African-American teachers and only a handful of African-American students. Adrift in a sea of white people, I felt alone, confused, and miserable.

When the other kids went out for recess, I made up all kinds of excuses to stay inside. There I would put my head down on my desk, reeling with anger, aching with the pain of loneliness. One day when I was inside during recess, Ms. G. came back to the classroom earlier than usual. Much to my surprise, she handed me a little blue book. Excellent at reading her students, Ms. G. knew how much I loved poetry. To my delight, she'd given me *The Dream Keeper* by Langston Hughes, one of my favorite poets.

The poems in this book were like precious pearls. I read one poem each day, impressing it into memory, into the very ground of my being. As I relished the poems, I realized that this was the first time in a classroom that I'd held a book of poems where the words had a cadence—that swing and sway—that sounded like the language I heard at home and at church. It was also the first time in a classroom where I'd opened a book with pictures of people who looked like me. People with eyes like mine. People with lips like mine.

When Ms. G. gave me Hughes' book, she thought she'd given me a book of poems. But what she really gave me was a long drink of water for my withered little soul. What she really gave me was a mirror, a mirror in which I could see myself and love myself just the way I was. This little blue book banished the mirrors of hatred and prejudice that were usually held before me. It banished the haters. It banished the bullies. With this little book, my sense of self was strengthened. Over time, my self-esteem soared.

Thank you, Ms. G., for making a way for me where there seemed to be no way.

Pass It On

How many of you have a Ms. G. in *your* life? A waymaker who became a beacon for you, providing you with a sense of validation and belonging at just the right time in your life?

Because I wanted to thank my teacher for the impact she'd made on my life, I spent a number of years and a fair amount of money searching for her. A couple of years ago, I finally found Ms. G. I'd sent her a letter through a third-party and asked her to call me when she received it.

Can you imagine what it's like to hear your teacher's voice after almost 50 years?

It made my soul sing!

Ms. G. and I spoke for well over an hour. We talked about so many things, sharing snippets of our lives. We laughed. We sang. And then she said something that made my heart stand still. "Gloria, no one but you has ever told me that I'd made a difference in their life."

I was stunned. How could that be? Over the years I'd kept in touch with a few of my classmates. When we met or saw one another during our high-school reunions, the one sure thing that brought joy and laughter was our shared, vivid memories of Ms. G.

"No one?"

"You are the only one, and I thank you."

What an honor it was to express my appreciation—to one of my heroes. Especially after all these years. And what an unexpected blessing to *receive* gratitudes from Ms. G.

In the weeks ahead, I reached out to my classmates to let them know I'd found Ms. G. With her permission, I shared her contact information with my friends. One by one, we connected to our beloved teacher, sharing our love and gratitude, building a bridge that connected us to the past and to the future.

Flawless Leadership **Practice**

Practice being a bridge builder.

Who has built a bridge or made a way for you?

Have you passed on what was given to you? Specifically, have you helped someone else by making a way or building a bridge for them?

If you haven't had an opportunity to do so, begin today. Ask yourself: *Who will I make a way for? Who will I build a bridge for?*

If you've already built a bridge or made a way for someone, bravo! Now, choose someone else and do it again...and again.

Make a "bucket list" of people for whom you can build a bridge. For each person, choose one thing that you learned that you can now pass on to make a difference in their life. Write it down.

Each week or month, choose someone else.

Over time, being a bridge builder will become first nature — an integral part of who you are.

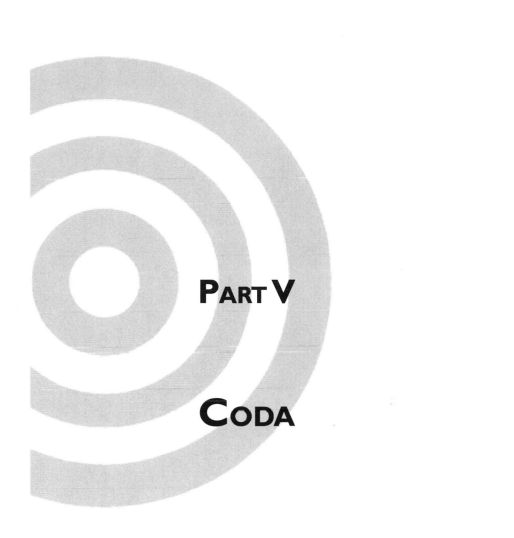

PART V

CODA

Yesterday I was clever, so I wanted to change the world.
Today I am wise, so I am changing myself.

JALAL-AD-DIN RUMI

Chapter 14

The Journey Continues

*No amount of human having or human doing
can make up for a deficit in human being.*

JOHN ADAMS

AS YOU REFLECT ON LEADERSHIP AND YOUR OWN LEADING, it is clear that connecting who you are with what you know and do will serve you well—in your organization, team, family, and any other context. In your quest to become the best leader you can be, there really is no end to developing and equipping yourself. This is truly a life-long journey. As you learn and develop, you will circle back through the same challenges, lessons, and opportunities, but you will do so at different altitudes and at different levels of awareness and ability.

As you continue on your leadership journey, you now have a toolkit. You can use this toolkit anytime, anywhere—now and forever. With it, you can tune into, bring forth, and develop the many dimensions of your being. As you explore and develop your being, you can revisit the same inner terrain, understanding that when you do so, you will experience it in a different way...not because the terrain has changed, but because you've changed.

The contents of your toolkit—new awareness and skills, qualities of being, questions, *Flawless Leadership* Practices, any notes you've jotted down—are valuable resources. These resources will support you by providing clarity, direction, and leverage. As you discover your purpose and follow your own North Star, these resources will support you on your journey now and in becoming the *flawless leader* you are meant to be.

A Poem for Your Journey

As an art form, poetry is singular. It is like no other. The presences in poems speak to us, revealing themselves in layers in their own time through our layers of being.

I often perform poems in my keynotes, during retreats with my clients, and in my workshops and seminars. I've had the opportunity to share "Song to Myself" with numerous audiences, and throughout the world this poem always strikes a deep chord. The presences speak to the leader that resides within each of us.

Because it's one of my most requested poems, I include it here as a resource for you and to share with others.

"Song to Myself" is a poem about faithfulness, responsibility, and service, a poem that resonates with the very heart of *flawless leadership*—connecting who you are with what you know and do.

Song to Myself

It doesn't matter to me
     what you do or where you work.
I want to know
     who you are
     when the sun goes down
     and if you are willing
     to put everything on the line
     to fulfill your soul's desire.

It doesn't matter to me
>   how much bread you can afford
>   to put on your own table.

I want to know
>   if you will knead and wait
>   and bake the bread and share
>   your blessings at someone else's table.

I want to know
>   if you can look into the eyes
>   of the young woman
>   who sleeps with fear each night
>   the one who dared to walk
>   away from the hands that pummeled her.

I want to know
>   if you can share her pain.

It doesn't matter to me
>   what neighborhood you live in
>   or what kind of car you drive.

I want to know
>   what drives you
>   what compels you
>   to follow your soul's longing.

I want to know
>   what pierces your heart
>   awakens you at night and inspires you
>   to devote yourself to whomever
>   or whatever moves you.

I want to know
>   how many times you've opened
>   your heart and extended a hand
>   to your homeless sister or brother.

I want to know
>   if you will sit in the quiet dark hours
>   between midnight and dawn listening
>   to another's heartsong.

It doesn't matter to me
      how many unspeakable secrets you have.
I want to know
      if you will share your secrets
      to liberate your demons
      so they don't devour you
      or those you love.
I want to know
      if you will risk looking foolish
      to embrace your bliss.
I want to know
      if you will grasp the sleeve
      of a nameless elder stumbling on his way
      and lead him in from the cold.
I want to know
      if you will throw away your cloak
      and show your heart if you will dare
      to wear your soul on the outside.

It doesn't matter to me
      how many mountains
      you've climbed or will climb.
I want to know
      if you've fallen down
      in the valley of despair.
I want to know
      if you've scarred your knees
      on the stones of self-abandonment.
I want to know
      how long you've been hidden in the shadows
      of hypocrisy prejudice addiction abuse.
I want to know
      if you will stop
      to light a candle and pray with others
      who will surely wander there.

It doesn't matter to me
        what you say you will do for others.
I want to know
        if you will act
        with courage and conviction
        if you will daily cradle the frail hand
        of your mother when she no longer
        knows your name.
I want to know
        if you will look into the hazel
        gray or ebony eyes of a stranger
        and say yes to affirm your sister
        your brother yourself.
I want to know
        if you will take the time to be still
        call the names and pass the cup
        to honor the ancestors
        who cleared a path
        and broke new ground
        for you and your children.

It doesn't matter to me
        that you have a past.
I want to know
        if you will celebrate your present
        if you will take a stand
        declare yourself sing I *am*
        boldly and with rejoicing
        not only to the stars at night
        but to anyone
        anywhere
        without apologies
        or regrets.

Works Cited

Bastian, E. Presentation delivered at an executive leadership conference, Atlanta, GA, 2014.

Beckett, S. *The Unnamable*, New York: Grove Press, 1958.

Bennis, W. *On Becoming a Leader*, New York: Perseus Books, 1989.

Block, P. *Flawless Consulting: A Guide to Getting Your Expertise Used*, San Francisco: Pfeiffer & Sons, 2000.

Burgess, G. *Dare to Wear Your Soul on the Outside: Live Your Legacy NOW*, San Francisco: Jossey-Bass, 2008.

Cameron, J. *Finding Water: The Art of Perseverance*, New York: Jeremy P. Tarcher/Penguin, 2006.

Campbell, J. *Reflections on the Art of Living: A Joseph Campbell Companion*, New York: Harper Perennial, 1995.

Cashman, K. *Leadership from the Inside Out: Becoming a Leader for Life*, Provo, Utah: Executive Excellence Publishing, 2000.

Csikszentmihalyi, M. *Flow: The Psychology of Optimal Experience*, New York: Harper and Row, 1990.

De Pree, M. *Leadership Jazz: The Essential Elements of a Great Leader*, New York: Dell Publishing, 1992.

Dillard, A. *The Writing Life*, New York: Harper and Row, 1989.

Dromgoole, W. A. "Building the Bridge," *Rare Old Chums*, Boston: E. P. Dutton and Company, 1898.

Elliott, W. *The Spiritual Life: Doctrine and Practice of Christian Perfection*, New York: New Paulist Press, 1914.

Hammergren, J. "Leadership Is About Values," McKesson.com.

Handel, G. F. Available at biography.com/people/george-handel-9327378.

Hesselbein, F. "The 'How to Be' Leader," *The Leader of the Future*, San Francisco: Jossey-Bass, 1996.

Keller, H. Available at afb.com/info/about-us/helen-keller/biography-and-chronology/biography/1235.

Maathai, W. *Unbowed: A Memoir*, New York: Anchor Books, 2007.

Mandela, N. *Long Walk to Freedom*, New York: Little Brown and Company, 1995.

Murray, W. H. *The Scottish Expedition*, London: J. M. Dent and Company, 1951.

O'Connor, S. Available at news.standford.edu/news/2004/june16/oconnor-text-616.htm.

PQ Blackwell Limited. *Believe: The Words and Inspiration of Desmond Tutu*, Boulder, Colo: Blue Mountain Press, 2007.

Schwarzkopf, H. N. *It Doesn't Take a Hero: The Autobiography of General H. Norman Schwarzkopf*, New York: Bantam, 1993.

Shaw, G. B. Available at elise.com/q/quotes/shawquotes.htm.

Southeast Alaska Traditional Tribal Values, 2004.

Sowcik, M. (ed). *Leadership 2050: Critical Challenges, Key Contexts, and Emerging Trends*, Bingley, England: Emerald Group Publishing, 2015.

Sweet, L. "A Learned to Learner Litany of Transformation," *Summoned to Lead*, Grand Rapids, Mich: Zondervan Publishing, 2004.

Van Wyck, C. *Nelson Mandela: Long Walk to Freedom*, New York: Roaring Brook Press, 2009.

Resources

THESE RESOURCES ARE FOR YOUR ONGOING learning, growth, and development. They have been and continue to be helpful to me, my clients, and my students.

Resources focused on writing will help you whether or not you write. Like writing, the journey of being is a spiritual journey. The poems and books that illuminate poetry and other aspects of creativity will also be helpful companions in your journey of connecting who you are with what you know and do. Why? Because poetry and other arts beckon us to slow down, to hit the pause button in our fast-paced lives. The arts also allow a sense of spaciousness in our otherwise crammed and cluttered lives. This quality of spaciousness soothes our soul while nourishing our being.

Bennis, W. *On Becoming a Leader*, New York: Perseus Books, 1989.

Bolman, L. and Deal, T. *Leading with Soul: An Uncommon Journey of Spirit*, San Francisco: Jossey-Bass, 1995.

Burgess, G. *Dare to Wear Your Soul on the Outside: Live Your Legacy NOW*, San Francisco: Jossey-Bass, 2008.

Burgess, G. *Legacy Living: The Six Covenants for Personal & Professional Excellence*, Provo, Utah: Executive Excellence Publishing, 2006.

Burgess, G. "Reflections on Leadership Formation and the Arts," in *The Wisdom of the Many: Key Issues in Arts Education*, edited by the International Network for Arts Education, Munich: Waxmann Publishing, 2015.

Burgess, G. "Song to Myself," *Journey of the Rose*, Edmonds, Wash: Jazz Media, 1998.

Carroll, K. *Rules of the Red Rubber Ball*, Bristol, Conn: ESPN, 2005.

Cashman, K. *Leadership from the Inside Out: Becoming a Leader for Life*, Provo, Utah: Executive Excellence Publishing, 2000.

Covey, S. M. R. and Merrill, R. *The Speed of Trust: The One Thing that Changes Everything*, New York: Free Press, 2006.

De Pree, M. *Leadership Jazz: The Essential Elements of a Great Leader*, New York: Dell Publishing, 1992.

Fritz, R. *Path of Least Resistance: Learning to Become the Creative Force in Your Own Life*, New York: Ballantine Books, 1989.

George, W. *True North: Discover Your Authentic Leadership*, San Francisco: Jossey-Bass, 2007.

Greenleaf, R. *Servant Leadership: A Journey into the Nature of Legitimate Power and Greatness*, Costa Mesa, Calif: Paulist Press, 1977.

Hesselbein, F. "The 'How to Be' Leader," *The Leader of the Future*, San Francisco: Jossey-Bass, 1996.

Hesselbein, F. (ed). "The Ultimate Task of Leadership," *The Leader of the Future*, San Francisco: Jossey-Bass, 1996.

Intrator, S. and Scribner, M. *Leading from Within: Poetry that Sustains the Courage to Lead*, San Francisco: Jossey-Bass, 2007.

Intrator, S. and Scribner, M. *Teaching with Fire: Poetry that Sustains the Courage to Lead*, San Francisco: Jossey-Bass, 2003.

Intrator, S. and Scribner, M. *Teaching with Heart: Poetry that Speaks to the Courage to Teach*, San Francisco: Jossey-Bass, 2014.

Kelly, M. *The Rhythm of Life: Living Every Day with Passion and Purpose*, New York: Simon & Schuster, 2004.

Kouzes, J. and Posner, B. *A Leader's Legacy*, San Francisco: Jossey-Bass, 2006.

Kunitz, S. "Touch Me," *Passing Through: The Later and New Poems*, New York: W.W. Norton and Company, 1995.

Maxwell, J.C. *The 21 Indispensable Qualities of a Leader: Becoming the Person Others Will Want to Follow*, Nashville, Tenn: Thomas Nelson, 2000.

Moore, T. (ed). *The Education of the Heart: Readings and Sources for the Care of the Soul, Soul Mates, and the Reenchantment of Everyday Life*, New York: Harper Collins, 1996.

Moon, J. *Stirring the Waters: Writing to Find Your Spirit*, Boston: Journey Editions, 2001.

Oliver, M. "The Summer Day," *The House of Light*, Boston: Beacon Press, 1990.

Palmer, P. *A Hidden Wholeness: The Journey Toward an Undivided Life*, San Francisco: Jossey-Bass, 2009.

Palmer, P. *Let Your Life Speak: Listening for the Voice of Vocation*, San Francisco: Jossey-Bass, 1999.

Parker, S. *212°: The Extra Degree*, Naperville, Illin: Simple Truths LLC, 2006.

Quinn, R. *Building the Bridge as You Walk On It: A Guide for Leading Change*, San Francisco: Jossey-Bass, 2004.

Rich, A. "Prospective Immigrants, Please Note," *Snapshots of a Daughter-in-Law*, New York: W.W. Norton, 1967.

Scharmer, O. *Theory U: Learning from the Future as It Emerges*, San Francisco: Berrett-Koehler, 2009.

Stengel. R. *Mandela's Way: 15 Lessons on Life, Love, and Courage*, New York: Crown Archetype, 2010.

Walcott, D. "Love After Love," *Sea Grapes*, New York: Farrar Straus Giroux, 1976.

Waldeman, D. *Remember Who You Are: Life Stories That Inspire the Heart and Mind*, Boston: Harvard Business School Press, 2004.

Wheatley, M. *Perseverance*, San Francisco: Berrett-Koehler, 2010.

Whyte, D. *Crossing the Unknown Sea: Work as a Pilgrimage of Identity*, New York: Riverhead Books, 2002.

The Author

GLORIA J. BURGESS, PHD, IS CEO OF Jazz International, an organization that inspires, develops, and equips leaders throughout the world. Gloria has served as a senior leader with diverse Fortune 100 companies, universities, and philanthropic organizations, including Adobe Systems, Bank of America, Citigroup, Honeywell, Xerox; University of Washington, Seattle Unversity, Saybrook University; and Casey Family Programs.

As a speaker, consultant, and executive coach, Gloria has presented keynotes, advised, and served numerous organizations and communities, including AT&T, Bill & Melinda Gates Foundation, Boeing, Equal Employment Opportunity Commission, Executive Women in Texas Government, Girl Scouts of America, International Coach Federation, Parliament of Kenya, Marguerite Casey Foundation, Microsoft, MSNBC, Paraguay's Office of the President, Providence Health and Services, Russell Investments, South African Embassy, and Starbucks.

Author of the best sellers *Legacy Living* and *Dare to Wear Your Soul on the Outside: Live Your Legacy NOW*, Gloria has also served as editor for two books in the International Leadership Association's prestigious Building Leadership Bridges series: *The Embodiment of Leadership* and *Leading in Complex Worlds*.

In addition to speaking, consulting, and coaching, Gloria is a professor. She serves as Visiting Faculty in programs for executive leaders at the University of Washington, University of Southern California (USC), and Seattle University. She has an MBA in Information Systems and Organizational Behavior from USC's Marshall School of Business. Gloria holds a PhD in Performance Studies from USC's Annenberg School for Communication and Journalism, and is a Distinguished Scholar in Theatre Direction and Performance.

A dynamic, inspiring speaker, Gloria presents keynotes on leadership, purpose, and passion for diverse audiences at corporate events and conferences around the world.

As speaker and evocateur, Gloria collaborates with her husband John on *Music for Transformation*™. Partnering with professional orchestras around the world, they design, create, and facilitate innovative learning experiences to surface key principles about diverse topics including leadership, collaboration, movement building, peacemaking, conflict resolution, diversity, inclusion, innovation, creativity, social artistry, empowerment, community building, and ecological sustainability. To learn more about John and Gloria's unique approach to learning through music and other arts, visit the website: www.johneburgess.com.

To learn more about Gloria's work, you can visit her website www.gloriaburgess.com or contact gloria@gloriaburgess.com.

Flawless Leadership Resources

LEARN HOW TO CONNECT WHO YOU ARE with what you know and do. Reach new heights in your personal and professional growth, performance, and results.

Gloria provides hands-on, interactive capacity building and skill building. She also delivers keynotes and provides individual and group coaching, mentoring, and training sessions for seasoned executives and emerging leaders.

Flawless Leadership 1—The Foundation

- Explore the Fundamentals of *Flawless Leadership*
- Discover Your Leadership Voice
- Discover What It Means and What It Takes to Be a *Flawless Leader*

Flawless Leadership 2—Discover Your WHY

- Identify Your Values
- Discover Your Purpose
- Create Your Personal Purpose Statement and Vision Map
- Learn the Competencies of *Flawless Leadership*
- Learn the Skills of *Flawless Leadership*

Flawless Leadership 3—Build Your Leadership Capacity

- Practice the Competencies of *Flawless Leadership*
- Practice the Skills of *Flawless Leadership*
- Apply the Competencies and Skills of *Flawless Leadership*

Other Workshops, Consulting, and Speaking:

- Leading from Within
- Leading with Purpose and Passion
- Leading from Success to Significance
- Legacy Leadership

We Equip, Inspire, and Transform
Leaders from the Inside Out.

To schedule, contact:

Phone: 206.954.0732

Email: info@gloriaburgess.com

Website: www.gloriaburgess.com

Mail: **Dr. Gloria Burgess**

c/o Jazz International

PO Box 777

Edmonds, WA 98020-0777

Index

A

Adams, John, 125
Adinkra circle, 4
Adinkrahene, 4
African blessing, 26
Angelou, Maya, 69
Authenticity, 12, 13, 88, 102. *See also* Faithfulness

B

Bastian, Ed, 30–32
Be a bridge builder, 115–122
  and building a bridge for others,
    116–117
  and making a way for others,
    119–120
  and mentors, 115–116
  and passing it on, 121
  Flawless Leadership Practice, 122
  how to, 119–120
Be a dreamer, 79–86
  and clarifying vision, 83–84
  and commitment, 81–82
  and putting wings on your dreams,
    81
  and working together, 80
  co-creating a future, 80
  example of, 81
  Flawless Leadership Practice, 86
  following your own vision, 84–85
  making things happen, 85–86
Be a learner, 95–103
  and being learned, 96–97
  and other cultures, 101–102
  and unlearning, 98–99
  and what it means, 96, 100
  as act of service, 97
  as growth, 98

  Flawless Leadership Practice, 102–103
  how to, 96–97
  through play, 100–101
Be a servant, 41–50
  and an attitude of serving, 42–44
  and a tribal model of service, 46–47
  and don't worry who gets the
    credit, 44–45
  and leader's role, 41
  and shifting focus, 45–46
  and values, beliefs, and practices of
    servant organizations, 48
  and valuing others, 49–50
  Flawless Leadership Practice, 49–50
Be courageous, 71–76
  and being audacious and daring,
    75–76
  and leading, 72–73
  and serving, 73–74
  Flawless Leadership Practice, 76
Be grateful, 19–27. *See also* Gratitude
  and appreciating others, 24–27
  and relationship to people, 20–21
  and relationship to place, 22–23
  and the influences of people, 20–21
  Flawless Leadership Practice, 27
  for the present, 23–24
Be inspired, 87–94
  and gathering inspiration, 88
  and surrendering to the flow, 88–89
  and *Ubuntu*, 90–92
  by shifting perspective, 89–90
  Flawless Leadership Practice, 93
Be intentional, 51–59
  and aligning with purpose, 55–57
  and beginning with the end in
    mind, 54–55
  and being on purpose, 57–58
  and identifying your values, 52–53
  be the change, 57–58

Flawless Leadership Practice, 58
  personal purpose statement, 54–55
Be persevering, 105–114
  a journey of recovery, 112
  and asking why not, 106
  and begin again, 112
  and qualities to possess, 106
  Flawless Leadership Practice, 113–114
  lessons from history, 107–110
Be the change, 57–58
Be trustworthy, 61–70
  and building trust one person at a
    time, 67–69
  and caring, 62, 63–64, 66
  and character, 62, 64–65, 66
  and competence, 62, 63, 66
  and consistency, 62, 65–66, 66
  and the essentials of building trust,
    62–66
    with caring, character,
    competence, consistency, 62–66
  Flawless Leadership Practice, 69–70
Be yourself, 29–37
  and curiosity, 32, 35–36
  and openness, 32, 33–34, 36
  and questions to ask yourself, 37
  and self-awareness, 32, 33, 36
  and transparency, 32, 34–35, 36
  Flawless Leadership Practice, 37
  skills needed, 30–36
Beckett, Samuel, 106
Beethoven, Ludwig von, 95
Behar, Howard, 65
Believe (PQ Blackwell), 91
Bennis, Warren, 8
Bolman, Lee, 39
"The Bridge Builder" (Dromgoole),
  116–117
Bridge building
  and Ms. G., 119–121
  and Pass It On, 121
  for others, 116–117
  one of greatest gifts, 115–116
"Building the Bridge" (Dromgoole),
  116–117
Burgess, Gloria
  and curiosity, 35–36
  and Dan, story of, 64
  and her mentors, 8, 35–36, 89–90,
    102, 119–121

and leadership formation, 20–23
and Ms. G., 119–120
and shifting perspective, 89–90
*Dare to Wear Your Soul on the
  Outside*, 44
on being yourself, 30
on caring, 64
on gratitude, 20, 21, 22–23
"Song to Myself," 127
Burns, Ursula, 63

C

Cameron, Julia, 87, 88
Campbell, Joseph, 29
Caring, 62, 63–64, 66, 69, 70
Carlisle, Donna, 5
Cashman, Kevin, 3
Character, 6, 64–65, 66, 69
Chávez, Favio, 118–119
Chenault, Kenneth, 54
Cherokee grandfather, story of,
  23–24. *See also* Two wolves, story of
Chesterton, G.K., 19
Churchill, Winston, 109–110
Cole, Johnnetta, 81
Commitment, 81–82, 84
Competence, 62, 63, 66, 69
Consistency, 65–66, 69
Courage
  being audacious and daring,
    75–76
  definition of, 72
  description of, 71
  to lead, 72–73
  to serve, 73–74
Csikszentmihalyi, Mihaly, 23
Curiosity, 12, 14–15, 32, 35–36, 100

D

Dale, story of, 7
Dan, story of, 64
Dare to Wear Your Soul on the Outside
  (Burgess), 44
Daskal, Lolly, 61
Deal, Terrence, 39
De Pree, Max, 19–20
Dillard, Annie, 51
Diversity, 13, 15, 48, 80

The Dream Keeper (Hughes), 120
Dromgoole, Will Allen, 116–117
Drucker, Peter, 5

E

Einstein, Albert, 81
Elliot, Walter, 105
Emmons, Robert, 25–26

F

Facets of leading
    knowing, doing, being, 4
Faithfulness, 12, 57, 102, 127
    and being authentic, 12, 13
    and being open and curious, 12, 14
    and integrity, 12, 13–14
    to purpose, 58
Finding Water (Cameron), 88
Flawless leadership
    aand trust, 62–66
    and being faithful, 12, 54, 63
    and building a bridge for others,
        118, 122
    and courage, 72–73, 75
    and delegating to others, 63
    and developing people, 21
    and emotional resonance, 33–34
    and hope, 15
    and humility, 88
    and inspiration, 88
    and intentional self-development,
        23
    and leading with intention, 51–52,
        58
    and life-changing questions, 9
    and life-long learning, 97, 100
    and living courageously, 75
    and making a way for others, 118,
        120, 122
    and perseverance, 106
    and presence, 23
    and purpose and intention, 15
    and refusal to accept status quo,
        106, 113
    and reliability and relationships, 65
    and serving others, 42–46, 97
    and skills to be yourself, 30–36
    and standing on values, 43, 58

    and surrender, 66
    and the gift within, 22–23
    and trust, 32
    and uncommon diligence, 106
    and unearthing and confronting
        lies, 97
    and unlearning, 97
    and vision, 32, 83–85
    and vulnerability, 66
    as a work in progress, 7
    key dimensions of, 11
Flawless Leadership Practice, 10, 27,
    37, 49–50, 58–59, 69–70, 76, 86, 93,
    102–103, 113–114, 122, 126
Flawless leadership resources, 139–140

G

Gandhi, Mahatma, 44
Gary, story of, 42–43
Gbowee, Leymah, 108
Ghana service-learning trip, 73–74
Gillespie, Mary Jane, story of, 119–121
Gómez, Nicolás, 118 119
Grace, story of, 43–44
Graham, story of, 102
Gratitude, 19, 88, 102. *See also* De Pree,
    Max
    and igniting positivity, 26–27
    and nourishing the heart and soul
        of community, 46
    and our relationship to people,
        20–21
    and our relationship to place,
        22–23
    as transformational, 24–27
    to focus our attention, 23–24
Gretchen, story of, 110–113

H

Haida tribe, 46–47
Hammergren, John, 52
Handel, George Frederick, 109
Heaney, Seamus, 80
Helen, story of, 67–69
Hesselbein, Frances, 1
Hoffer, Eric, 96
Hope, 12, 15
Hughes, Langston, 120

I

Imagination, 81, 86
Inspiration
 and change of scenery, 89–90
 begins with humility, 88
Inspire
 definition of, 87
Integrity, 11, 12, 13–14, 48, 102
Intention, 51, 52, 53, 81, 84
 and Nelson Mandela, 57–58

J

Jin, story of, 55–57
Jobs, Steve, 109
Journey of becoming, 8, 33–34, 84, 86, 113, 125–126
 from HERE to THERE, 117

K

Keller, Helen, 107–108
Kennedy, Rosemary, 108
King, Martin Luther, Jr., 44

L

Landfill Harmonic Orchestra, 118–119. *See also* La Orquesta de Instrumentos Reciclados de Cateura; Los Reciclados
La Orquesta de Instrumentos Reciclados de Cateura, 118–119. *See also* Landfill Harmonic Orchestra; Los Reciclados
Leaders
 and authenticity, 13
 and cultivating relationships, 63–64
 and curiosity, 35–36
 and dependence on others, 20
 and faithfulness, 12
 and hope, 15
 and integrity, 13–14
 and making things happen, 63
 and openness, 14–15, 33–34
 and reliability, 65–66
 and revealing character, 64–65
 and self-awareness, 32
 and standing on broad shoulders, 106
 and transparency, 34–35
 as servants, 43–44
 develop from inside out, 4
 non-positional, 75–76, 80
 positional and non-positional, 112–113
 positional vs. non-positional, 75–76
Leadership
 accountability, 13
 and being, 4
 and servant-leadership, 22, 45, 93
 as a process of becoming, 8
 formation, 3–4
 journey, 8, 125–126
 personal leadership, 5–6
 toolkit, 125–126
Leadership 2050 (Sowcik, M., ed.), 79
Leadership Jazz (De Pree), 19
Leading
 facets: knowing, doing, being, 4
 from the inside out, 4, 22–23, 54, 110
 from within, 3
"A Learned to Learner Litany of Transformation" (Sweet), 96
Learning
 and curiosity, 36
 and unlearning, 98–99
 as act of service, 97
 as growth, 98
 from other cultures, 101–102
 through play, 100–101
Life-Changing Questions, 8–10
 How will I channel my passion to serve others?, 9–10, 77
 What is unique about me?, 9–10, 17, 54
 Who and what do I care about?, 9–10, 39, 54
Los Reciclados, 118–119. *See also* Landfill Harmonic Orchestra; La Orquesta de Instrumentos Reciclados de Cateura

M

Maathai, Wangari, 11, 108–109
Madame Butterfly (Puccini), 88
Mandela, Nelson, 44–45, 57–58, 71, 72

and Mphakanyiswa, Gadla Henry, 57
and Uncle Jongintaba, 57
as Rolihlahla, 57
Marshall, Thurgood, 20
Maxwell, John C., 64
McLaughlin, Mignon, 72
Mead, Margaret, 17
Michelangelo's *David*, 89
Mother Teresa, 44
Ms. G. *See* Gillespie, Mary Jane, story of
Murray, W. H., 82

N

Negro spiritual
Gospel Plow, 23

O

O'Conner, Sandra Day, 115
Omar, story of, 100–101
One Hat Theory of Leadership, 65
Openness, 11, 12, 14–15, 32, 33–34, 36
Orquesta de Instrumentos Reciclados de Cateura. *See* La Orquesta de Instrumentos Reciclados de Cateura

P

Passion, 9, 10, 55, 77, 107–110
Pass It On, 121
Patton, George S., 72
Pearl, story of, 44–45
Perseverance
lessons of, 110
Perseverer
lessons from history, 107–110
qualities of, 106
Personal leadership, 5–6
Personal mastery, 36. *See also* Self-awareness; Openness; Transparency; Curiosity
Personal purpose statement, 54–55
Peter, story of, 72–73
Practice. *See Flawless Leadership* Practice
Puccini, Giacomo, 88
Purpose, 10, 51, 54–58, 67, 74, 84, 86, 107–110, 112, 119, 126
aligning with work, 55–57

and being in harmony with, 84
and being the change, 57–58
life's story as, 113

Q

Qualities of being, 7, 10, 12, 110, 126
Be a bridge builder, 115
Be a dreamer, 79
Be a learner, 95
Be a servant, 41
Be courageous, 71
Be grateful, 19
Be inspired, 87
Be intentional, 51
Be persevering, 105
Be trustworthy, 61
Be yourself, 29

R

Raj, story of, 25
Rare Old Chums (Dromgoole), 116
Reciclados. *See* Los Reciclados
Responsibility, 127
Rhea, story of, 99–100
Roosevelt, Eleanor, 44
Rumi, Jalal-ad-Din, 123

S

Schwarzkopf, H. Norman, 65
Schweitzer, Albert, 44
Self-awareness, 13, 32, 33
Servant-leadership, 22, 45, 93
Service, 43, 45, 49–50, 88
and being intentional, 51–52
and "The Bridge Builder" poem, 117
and compassion, generosity, knowledge, and wisdom, 42
and courage, 73
and Dale's story, 7
and Gloria Burgess' story, 36
and Grace's story, 43–44
and Graham's story, 102
and Gretchen's story, 111–113
and having been served by others, 45
and Helen's story, 67–69

and hope, 15
and learning as act of, 97
and learning from other cultures
   and traditions, 46–48
and Nelson Mandela, 44–45
and passion, 9, 10, 77
and Pearl's story, 44
and servant-leadership, 22, 45, 93
and servant organizations, 48
and "Song to Myself" poem, 127
and Sumaya's story, 74
and the military, 41–42, 109
and tribal model, 46–47
and your values, 52–53
as core value, 7
combined with passion, 111
exemplars of, 44
in organizations and communities,
   43
Shackleton, Ernest, 107
Shaw, George Bernard, 97
Shriver, Eunice Kennedy, 108
Sirleaf, Ellen Johnson, 44, 108
"Song to Myself" (Burgess), 127
Southeast Alaska Traditional Tribal
   Values chart, 47
Sullivan, Anne, 107–108
Sumaya, story of, 74
Sweet, Leonard, 96

T

Three Life-Changing Questions.
   See Life-Changing Questions
Tlingit tribe, 46–47
Transparency, 32, 34–35, 36
A tribal model of service, 46–47
Trust
   and building, 67–69
   declaration of dependence, 66
   declaration of interdependence, 66
   earning and sustaining, 62
   essentials of building, 62–66
Trustworthiness, 61–62
   and demonstrating it to others, 66–68

Turner, Etta, 29
Tutu, Desmond, 91–92
Twain, Mark, 55
Two wolves, story of, 23–24. *See
   also* Cherokee grandfather, story of
Tyner, Artika R., 77

U

Ubuntu, 90–93
   and Desmond Tutu, 91–92
   definition of, 91–92
   story of, 92

V

Value Others chart, 49
Values, 6, 67, 102
   and being authentic, 13
   identifying, 52–53, 58–59
   questions to identify, 52–53
   to create purpose statement, 54–55
Values, attitudes, and beliefs, 6
Values, beliefs, and practices list, 48
Vision. *See also* Be a dreamer; Be
   inspired
   act on plan, 85
   being in harmony with purpose, 84
   clarifying, 83–84
   connecting to, 84
   take step towards, 84
   turn into plan, 85

W

Ward, William Arthur, 41
Who you are, 3–6
   and being, 4
   and leadership formation, 3
   and leading from within, 3
   as a facet of leading, 4
   essence of leadership, 5
   values, attitudes, and beliefs, 6
Wright Brothers, 107